Keke

Keke

Keke Rosberg
and Keith Botsford

Stanley Paul

London Melbourne Sydney Auckland Johannesburg

Stanley Paul & Co. Ltd

An imprint of the Hutchinson Publishing Group

17–21 Conway Street, London W1P 6JD

Hutchinson Publishing Group (Australia) Pty Ltd
16–22 Church Street, Hawthorn, Melbourne, Victoria 3122

Hutchinson Group (NZ) Ltd
32 34 View Road, PO Box 40 086, Glenfield, Auckland 10

Hutchinson Group (SA) Pty Ltd
PO Box 337, Bergvlei 2012, South Africa

First published 1985
© Keke Rosberg and Keith Botsford 1985

Set in Garamond by Book Ens, Saffron Walden, Essex

Printed and bound in Great Britain
by Anchor Brendon Ltd, Tiptree, Essex

ISBN 0 09 156180 9

Contents

Acknowledgements

For permission to reproduce copyright photographs, the authors and publishers would like to thank David Winter, Steve Yarnell, Foto Opte oy and Nigel Snowdon.

Introduction

Not the most glamorous driver in the world. One French journalist, stuck well in a past that's long-gone, says, Rosberg, who's he? He's only won one race in his career! All right, so it's three. Three hard-won, two of them in a car that had to be wrestled to the finish line.

Keke has his detractors. There are reasons for this. The first is that he does not suffer fools gladly. The second is that he says what he thinks and the world be damned. The third is that he likes money and admits it. The fourth is that he's a loner. The fifth is . . . You could go on and on.

The image of the man is: a canary-yellow set of overalls, a golden moustache, mirror sunglasses, a cigarette in hand, a beautiful wife. All of them combine – together with homes hither and yon, Maidenhead, Ibiza, Austria – to create an impenetrable front.

Why should I bare my soul? I'm a paid driver, that's what I do in life. I'm not a philosopher.

From a non-philosopher – and a man who admits to being profoundly lazy off the track – you're not going to get a coherent story. Drivers are a great source of obiter dicta. *Of the off-the-cuff. We spent many hours, in Brazil, in Ibiza, in Detroit and on circuits all around the world, talking to each other, but, apart from racing, almost everything that goes through a driver's mind is improvised on the spot. It comes out in short, snappy bursts. It tells its own tale. You get vignettes of a real life somewhere behind the explanations, the attempts to wrestle with real thoughts, the detailed accounts of manoeuvres well in the past but alive and real to the man.*

There are lots of ways to arrange a driver's book, his life – his art, if you like. Any attempt to put too much order on his raw material is misleading. The raw material wasn't put together that way. Driving at the very top is a matter of accretion. Little bits of experience pile on other little bits, learning is constant, disaster always just around the corner. Drivers are not sprung, full-blown, from fast kids in go-karts.

All the writer can do is dig, dig some more and then dig again. The nuggets will come up, but with as much effort as though you were mining for coal in the Mindanao Deep. Drivers don't really want to reveal themselves. That way lies vulnerability. They are as superstitious as nineteenth-century Africans facing a camera and thinking the photographer will walk away with their souls.

This, therefore, is an anthology of Keke. Of things put in his own way. At the end, there is a composite Keke. A composite Keke is the quintessential modern driver: a Lauda, a Prost, a Piquet, any of his peers. At that level, the peers are never more than a handful.

Keke represents what Formula One is today. You may not like what the sport has become, but if you listen to Keke you'll know a lot more about its reality than you will by reading someone puffing himself up (or more often being puffed up by a ghostly parasite). That French journalist, for instance. His resentment is perfectly straightforward. His memories are of Jim Clark, of Fangio, of mythical heroes long gone, of men who raced in a different age, with different cars and different pressures, with different attitudes and different responsibilities. It just ain't that way no more. It's hard, cruel and very professional. The survivors are the best pros, the most complete drivers, the most self-aware, hard-nosed SOBs. Being exploited, they know how to exploit. They don't give you a used Kleenex without payment. What they drink, what they wear, what they drive, what they play tennis with are all paid for by someone who wants something from them.

That's sport?

No, it's commerce.

The sport survives because some people in it care deeply about it, about the sport *of it. Not for a minute forgetting to get from Mammon their due.*

Keke, what is a professional?

Being a professional is looking after your own bloody future. No one else is going to look after it for you.

Is that really so different from any other sport, or any other profession? Drivers might think they are independent, but they're not. They're dependent on teams, on cars, on luck.

F1 only employs ten to fifteen drivers a year. The rest, whatever they say, have a great desire and supply their own machines. So obviously it's different; it's a tough world at the top. That only makes you want to climb Everest that little bit more.

And once up there, you're not scared of falling off the top? Which is what your team manager, Frank Williams, said kept him going.

I agree. I work hard because I don't want ever to fall back into what it was like before I got to the top. I don't look back much, anyway; but then I also don't think I'm on top. I'm not on top *now*, am I? I think I can reach that top only by working harder. Or, to put it another way, I think that by working harder I can reach more and more. I don't mean make more money. I mean I can get closer to what it is I'm possessed by and we're all possessed by.

I have a very big inner drive. I'm very hungry. That's what keeps me going, not the fear of falling back into the lower reaches.

At first, it might be the fear of falling; in the end, it isn't – it's an appetite to be the best. Hundreds of strands make up the driver's life.

1

From Birth to Bikes

His parents both raced. Father Lasse was a veterinary surgeon (now retired) and Mother a chemist; they raced all over Finland, where they returned after the birth on 6 December, 1948 of Keijo Erik in Stockholm, when both parents were students.

Very young, Keke sat in the family Ford, turned the ignition key and the car advanced, wobbling, towards the garage door while Keke, terrified, clung to the steering wheel. The car, says Keke's father, still bears traces of its mishap – and of Keke's first ride.

Later Keke got a bike and pedalled it at the head of the May Day parade, among the red flags. At a kids' competition, he won his first race; the prize was a pair of ping-pong bats.

That was in Hamina. In Oulu, where the family moved when Keke was nine, his racing-crazy parents supported the building of the first go-kart track. Keke tried it out, liked it. He was, alas, six years short of a licence to race. Son accompanied father. 'We were a touching tandem,' says the father. The family moved to Iisalmi and two years later Keke borrowed a motorbike to get his licence. Father and son raced in Lahti in the spring of 1965. It was the father's last race and Keke's first.

Beginnings

Maybe it is appropriate, since the Finns descend supposedly from the Mongol hordes, that Keke should have started his career in Formula One with Teddy Yip and his Theodore team in 1978. Teddy had a lot of things that made him stand out in Formula One, but most of all, he actually enjoyed going racing – a luxury few team owners can permit themselves these days. The origins of Teddy's money are fairly obscure. Some say he made some good deals in Burma during the last war. It might be true. He's old enough and smart enough. But at least it was his money in the team. Not a sponsor's. That made the atmosphere around Teddy and his cars quite particular. His motor-

home was as modest as the Chinese logo on the front of his car. In later years he appeared with his son, a babe in arms; Teddy was then, some said, into his eighties. He was the opposite of the Chinese cliché: he was the most scrutable of men. Written on his face was a love of good times, good drink, charming women and good companionship. He raced for several years in Formula One but his cars never made it.

A super bloke. He asked Eddie Cheever to drive for him before he asked me, but Eddie turned the drive down, thinking a Chinese team wasn't good enough for him. I jumped quick. There aren't that many ways for a Finn to get into F1.

That is undoubtedly true. There are racing countries and there are countries where they race and develop good drivers, but the odds on getting the right sponsorship, on having access to the teams, on having enough practice in other formulas, on having enough friends in the business, are against drivers who are not English, French, German or Italian. Brazilians make it, but they have to emigrate to Europe to do so, as did Reutemann from Argentina.

The reasons are simple. To get into Formula One you have to be noticed. *It's hard to get noticed in some countries, especially those which do not have a Grand Prix of their own. The fact that Sweden has one is one reason why Ronnie Peterson made it, or why Stefan Johansson will. But in Finland it's rallies. Dozens of Finns rally and dominate the world championship. To go the other route takes persistence, tenacity, a clear sense of purpose and a bit of luck.*

I have to laugh at all those young English, French and Italian drivers crying over how hard it is to get into F1. The biggest single-seater race we ever had in Finland was an F3 race. Finns have no opportunity to expose themselves, to be seen. Like Canadians – yet Gilles Villeneuve made it to the top. He made it because Marlboro were interested in him, even though they don't have a market in Canada, because he was good. But no one was interested in me.

Anyway, when Eddie said no, Sid Taylor, who ran the team for Teddy, called me. He knew me from F2 and probably even more from Formula Atlantic.

I didn't make any big conditions. I said I'd have to be paid to drive. That's all. Because I make my living out of motor racing – though at the time I didn't. I wasn't like some of the current hot shots who think they ought to be paid a fortune to sit in a car. England's Jonathan Palmer took the same road last year: he found his own backing and got into F1, not to make bread but to get his chance. At that time, for me, the most important thing was to get into F1 and then to make enough money in it to be able to live: travel, pay my rent, go racing and give myself a chance. A thousand dollars a race: that's what you could buy Rosberg for in 1978. It was a bit more than I got in F2 and that was fine: that's what I asked for and that's what I got.

I owe Sid Taylor for getting me the drive, but not for much else. I never had any problems with Teddy Yip, or with the mechanics. But there were clashes on the team management side. The team wasn't being run as it should have been. It wasn't my job to tell Sid how to run the team, but I'd just got into F1 and it was crucial for me. Besides, I tend to say what I think. And even if you don't have much money for the team, you can still try to do things as well as possible.

But because of my arguments I got a black ball from the team and I'm not sure that Teddy knew how much I appreciated him. Sid was OK as a man, but he was no team manager. There was this father–adopted son relationship between Sid and Teddy, but Teddy was way over Sid's head. I've never met anyone with such incredible energy. He was in a bad period then – he was drinking a lot – but you look at him now, he's born again!

I always felt sorry for Teddy. He brought money into F1 and his only reward was a headache. Everything that could go wrong always went wrong. With the money he put into his team he could have been a sponsor, a manager, a backer with any team, enjoyed his racing and gone back to his business. But I think Sid gave him poor advice. Sid wanted him to have his own team. Maybe Teddy got the kicks out of it he wanted; at least Yip can say he had a lot of good drivers go through his hands: Patrick Depailler, Nelson Piquet, Alan Jones . . .

The second race I drove for him was the Silverstone International, a really dirty race because of the rain. I was covered in mud, but I had won. As I was going up on the podium, Teddy handed me an immaculate silk handkerchief with which to wipe my face. I promptly muddied it and threw it away without thinking. When I got back to the motor-home, I said, 'Shit, Teddy, I've lost your handkerchief!' He said, 'Thank God! An old Chinese superstition says, if someone gives you a handkerchief, whatever you do, don't keep it!'

I only raced from March to August with him, but he was one of the last really to love his racing. Always busy, he was also always approachable. Straightforward, no tricks. A thousand dollars a race doesn't sound so great, but it was a living. I was living well. I've always lived well from motor racing. Maybe I didn't save millions back in 1976–77, but I had no complaints.

I also had my own business things going from the start. They gave me the chance to get out of Finland but also to keep my contacts back home.

Nowadays, it's different. We read that drivers are refused a drive because the $350,000 they bring to the team is insufficient.

Hell, if I'd had that sort of money, I'd have retired. Or I would have offered $50,000 to the team, which would have been better for them than paying me $10,000. I've never had to bring money into a team. I had sponsors who helped me get going; I had the bread from the team and I could buy the butter on what my personal sponsors gave me. Maybe, too, there was someone who sent me free sausages so I could eat a proper breakfast. That was the size of it back then and I was very grateful. I was able to do the kind of work I wanted to do and live from it. I made out. In 1975 I bought my own brand-new Jag. In 1978 I bought a Mercedes. I thought it was great for a Finn to be able to ride around in a big Mercedes. It wasn't the status; it gives me great pleasure to drive a car like that. I had my penthouse in Germany. I loved it.

I wasn't doing all that on $1000 a race. I was racing every weekend or doing something else. It's the bread-and-butter theory: the bread from racing, the butter from elsewhere.

A man who travels a great deal doesn't have much time left in which to spend money. I've saved money all my racing life. From the way I live, people think I'm a big spender. It's not so. I spend less, a lot less, than most people who have the kind of income I have. Back then, I used to borrow money; it's a good way of saving. It forces you to control yourself, not go overboard. I've always paid my debts and I've never fallen on my arse. I've always lived within my limits.

Inside Keke, as inside many another modern driver, two motives dominate: one is the need to drive and the need for the pleasure it gives; the other is desire for money and the satisfaction it brings. The driver, like the artist or the performer, is as near to being a self-made man as you can get. Even if you are born rich, or very rich like Elio de Angelis, there is no possibility of becoming what you want to become without achieving it yourself. Achieving is making yourself, forging your identity. Elio probably enjoys his share of the prize money more than his share in the family business. This is all the more true if you start from nowhere, or nearly nowhere, and make it to the top.

The social stratum from which racing drivers derive has altered radically in the last ten years. Not all the drivers of the so-called Golden Age (which is always further back than anyone can remember properly) were 'gentlemen'. But the majority had means of one sort or another; even if they lacked the ultimate talent, they had the means to display such talent as they had. But without talent, today's driver is a non-starter. He may bring one or two million dollars to a team, but ultimately he's still a millstone about its neck.

Money will get you into racing; it will keep you in racing for a while; it can't do more for you than that. Not having money can keep you out of racing at the start; if you have talent, it won't keep you out of it for ever; it will only delay you, as it did Keke. But the key to the modern driver is that you can hardly think of the racing without thinking of the money. The two today are inextricably connected. Racing and money. Money and racing. To admit this is in many people's mind a crime.

Keke seems to have seen this early. If racing was the motive, money was in part the end. Or vice versa, if the money was the motive, racing was the goal? I once asked him if racing on its own satisfied him.

No, just turning the wheel doesn't satisfy me. One of the things that most fascinates me about motor racing is the marketing side of it.

16

In the seventies, when Keke started, the sport had just been professionalized – shall we say, commercialized? Jackie Stewart was a trailblazer. The effect of his slow, careful exploitation of his championships made itself felt all the way down the sport. Even kids could understand, as the spirit in sport in general changed – as tennis players went pro, as footballers began to earn large sums, as performers' managers and agents came into being – that money which is the visible side of success was now a part of sport. And if you weren't born rich, there was one way you could get rich, and fairly quickly: you could exploit your own talents to the extreme. Turn your tennis racquet from pleasure to profit. You need not even lose, altogether, the pleasure in the sport. But you needed to be a lot harder with yourself. You had to forego a lot to claw your way to the top. Forget your personal life, forget – if you ever cared about it – education, culture, family. If you were lucky, you could come back to that.

Thus Keke looked at what was going on around him and realized that, while he loved racing above all else, he had to make a living, and that a living was to be made out of doing what he loved best. And that the better he did it, the better living he would have. And to become as good as that, it was unthinkable to remain an amateur.

It started early. I was racing go-karts and I couldn't understand why I should be riding go-karts and paying for it. I was paying too much. I couldn't afford to do it the way I wanted. I could afford to go round in circles, but I couldn't *compete*. I wasn't prepared to stay at that level and enjoy it. Success was more important, and still is. So I decided to quit go-karts and go into motor racing. And having looked at the sport, I was convinced that I could get other people to pay for my pleasure. It sounds awful, but that's how it started. That's why I bought an FVee car. I didn't buy it with the idea of becoming an F1 champion. I bought it because I wanted to go racing, because I loved to go racing. What I wanted was to become a dentist, because I saw that if I became a dentist, I couldn't afford to go racing. Maybe that's why I failed my exams.

Not once, but twice, as it happens. But even then, the manner of it was typically Keke: a little aslant.

17

The first time I took those exams, I simply lost interest. There was a six-week course. I spent all six weeks in the swimming pool.

The second time, I took them seriously, because I knew I wouldn't get another chance: six weeks of chemistry and biology, and I really studied. I had managed to get myself out of my military service for three months so I could study. It was the first time in my life apart from motor racing that I really worked; I wanted to score maximum points. I did so in the first exam. Unfortunately, I didn't wake up for the second.

It's always been a running joke, my sleep. I sleep that deeply, I'm unconscious. I'll miss a Grand Prix one day through not waking up. On my own, I'm hopeless. I have to have someone to wake me up. When I was a kid, I gave my father heart attacks. I should have left for school at 7.45, but I left at four minutes to the hour. And still made it. At the very last second. It was stupid. I made my life hectic for nothing. It's not that I liked living dangerously: quite seriously, those extra minutes of sleep were worth it. Worth more than all the gold in the world.

I was living in a flat in Helsinki and although my mother had come down for a week to help out so I could study, she didn't know that I was taking the exam that day. I studied until five, fell asleep and woke up after nine, which was when the exam started. They let you in until half past. Well, I broke every traffic regulation in the world getting there, I jammed the car in front of the door and ran up the stairs, and there was the guard at the top saying, 'I'm sorry, we locked the doors five minutes ago.' I felt sick; I'd blown my future for five minutes. You have to score a certain number of points and without the second exam I couldn't possibly make it. I didn't feel stupid: but my world had collapsed, and what were my parents going to say?

You see, money always comes into it. My father had to give up racing because he didn't have enough money. In fact, my mother gave it up first. Then they went to great expense on my go-kart career, not so much on equipment, but on travel. We went to Paris for the world championship, to Turin for the European. That's a hell of a long way from Finland when you're doing it in your own car during the holidays.

Racing was in my father's blood. When he finished his studies, the first thing he did was get into motor sport. It was easier in those days; even rallying was simpler. Then, like the rest of motor sport, it suddenly got very expensive and my father dropped out.

But what he went through enabled him to understand the way I felt about racing; at the same time, he knew the dangers of getting involved.

When I bought my first racing car, he wouldn't talk to me for a year. When I called home, he'd say, 'Mum, it's your son calling.' That's how hard he took it, because I wasn't listening to his advice. He thought I was being bloody stupid because I only had a tiny income as a computer trainee and there I was getting into a sport he *knew* could get to be like a drug. He didn't want me to go down the same road as he had: getting hooked and then having to give it up because I didn't have the money to go racing. I'd failed my exams, I was starting in a new field I didn't fully understand. In his eyes, I was destroying myself. I had debts up to my ears, a lovely house I hadn't paid for, I was the proud owner of a trailer and a Mustang with a big V/8 engine in it, hand-styled.

I can see his point. He didn't want me to destroy my financial future and he didn't want me to be miserable when it came to giving up racing. He wanted to protect me from getting hurt.

I didn't believe him. I said the kind of things kids say. The times have changed. I know it's too expensive for me but I can pay it off. He generously lent me £150 towards the first car and the bank gave a little. I had a little. Still, the whole season, he wouldn't talk to me.

Maybe he also saw how naive I was. I simply believed in myself, as though that was all you needed to go racing. I knew nothing whatever about the technical side of motor sport. In go-karting, my mechanic was a vet. He just about knew that you grabbed a screwdriver by the thick end. I won pole position in the karting world championship with an engine that had been rebuilt five times in a week's testing; it seized up every day we went out. I didn't know much more about the technique of driving, either. If my kart understeered, I thought all I had to do was drive it differently.

Looking back, I can see the point my dad was trying to make. I had neither adequate finance nor any knowledge of how to set up a car or improve it. We couldn't go testing. We had one or two engines while other people had twenty. If the car didn't behave, all I could do was drive harder.

Still, I got to my first race. I parked my FVee in the paddock. Next to me was a guy called Jussi Varjosaari. He'd started racing that spring as well. He walked around the car which I'd bought only two days before and painted so as it looked nice. 'You really prepared it for this race,' he said to me, shaking his head sadly. I could see what he was thinking: This bloke's got no idea what he's doing. Then he said, 'Why don't you go away for two hours? Just stay away, will you?' And when I came back, he had prepared the car.

He remains one of my best friends, even though I beat him in that first race. He knows there are things I simply cannot do. He's good with his hands and I'm not. He tried very hard, but he never made it as a driver.

I think I was different. Even at that first race I had a sponsor. If you'd asked me at fifteen what I wanted to do, and be, I'd have said, 'Be sixteen and go karting.' There would have been no point saying I was going to be an F1 driver. The difference is that I've always been very realistic. Today I am an F1 driver because I was always very realistic about the difficulties in getting there.

I learned early. As I said, I realized I could get other people to pay for my fun. I saw that clearly before I bought my first car. My first season in FVee cost me nothing. I didn't make anything but I didn't lose anything. I was very proud of that. My main sponsor never paid me and still I broke even.

Youth and Age

Formula One is a summit that you reach relatively late in your career. Entry is not easy, success is slow to come. In the 1985 championship Keke will be the most senior driver in the field. 'Quick when young' is a tagword in his vocabulary. Quick when young, wise when old? It is hard to imagine that Keke has in any way slowed down.

That's how I made it in the first place: by being quick. I was a young, very fast driver. If the car had three wheels, I'd still drive it. Today, if the angle of a wheel is slightly off, I drive it into the pits. Because I am not prepared to take risks. The difference is that I now know that it hurts, to take risks. Back then, I didn't.

A young driver can make it, but by the time he gets to F1 he's not likely to be so young any more. And very few young drivers, say at twenty-one or twenty-two, have the maturity of mind to put in a whole competitive season. They can do a one-off and make an impression, but they can't fight against the odds and keep up the pace through a whole year.

A mature mind uses its experience and knowledge; it can think out a season; it can see the season as a whole and realize that every day counts towards the whole package. What does a young driver know about completeness? His whole life is a series of moments.

I don't care how talented you are, it takes at least two years to make a Grand Prix driver out of someone entering F1. It is so much more complicated than we think when we come into F1. To be fast – great! But everyone who comes in is fast, or else they wouldn't be there. To build a Grand Prix driver out of someone who is merely quick takes a long time. A young driver might win one race, but can he maintain his performance throughout the season? Does he know how to treat the car properly? Has he got the right work habits, the right attitude? Can he develop his car and everything that involves? Does he know how to nurse a car home when it is about to fall to pieces?

At thirty-five, Keke thinks he is at the right age for the job. The right age for him, because he started late and developed late; but also in a more general sense, that drivers need something extra gained from age and maturity before they are any good at their job.

What still hits me about F1 is that it matures you so quickly. It is the best form of character building in the world. Mainly because in F1 you learn to take the bad with the good. Up to that point you've been moving up through the ranks; you can see progress; you're getting better at your job; more and more people recognize your talents. Then you're in F1 and you've supposedly made it; only to realize that you haven't made anything at all.

You have to start all over again, from the very beginning. The young find it hard to cope with the sheer frustration.

Driving an F1 car is painful. For me it is sheer physical strain. I can think of no other sport in the world which is so punishing. But I love to push myself to the extreme. I love to see how far I can push my body, how much it will take. I like to go up on the podium and there I am, fresh; the other drivers are falling all over the place, Nelson Piquet throwing up in his helmet in Brazil. It's all part of having a psychological edge. The stronger you are physically, the stronger you are mentally. You don't come into this sport that strong. It's something you learn and develop. If you don't, you'll never make it.

I can't remember a Grand Prix in which I haven't seen someone slipping just because of lack of physical or mental condition. I sit behind them and I can see their concentration going. That's a product of mental and physical exhaustion. Two hours is a very long time. No outsider knows just how long it is.

The young lack the stamina. They aren't ready to accept that at Monaco there is not a microsecond of rest. The mind has to react, to think ahead, to observe, to plot for every fraction of every second.

Experience is a help. Concentration becomes a habit. When you start in Formula Vee or F3, ten laps seems like the end of the world; they leave you completely exhausted, as exhausted as seventy laps in F1. It is horrifying to the beginner. But when you analyse it you come to see that much of your exhaustion or your stamina depends on your attitude towards the race. Are you an attacker by nature? Or are you the sort of driver who sits and waits?

Niki is the sort who sits and waits. He doesn't need to put as much energy into his driving as some others. He knows his pace; he knows what pace suits his car; he has learned limits. That's experience. People think Niki was always like that, but when he was young he was as far from that as you can get. The young lack the patience to wait.

Me, I run on the very edge of endurance throughout a race. I fight against the car and against myself all the time. I'm sure I don't *need* to do it like that. It just happens to be my nature. I'm made like that and although I have the experience, I can't find a way of altering the basic facts about myself.

I thought that when I'd won the championship I'd change; I'd no longer have anything to prove. I thought I would be pleased, relaxed. Maybe it's the fear of falling back. A year in a Cosworth-powered engine when all the rest were in turbos is fall enough! So why didn't I just relax and cruise around the tracks? I don't know. I know it's in my nature to fight.

Coming into F1 is also a huge psychological leap from whatever you were doing before. It was for me. I'm a Finn, not an Englishman. An Englishman has grown up with F1 before he's ever driven a race. Finland is not an F1 country and I only started reading about it when Ronnie Peterson started racing in F1, and then only because I'd known Ronnie in karting. The rest of the people were just names to me. When I started karting Ronnie was already in a different league. I did my first world championship race when he did his last. I didn't know him well, though we had quite a bit of contact. What was important about Ronnie for me was that he was in a privileged position: he was racing cars.

I didn't ask myself whether I was as good as he was. I just went ahead in my own way; each step came as it came. For someone from the middle of Finland, F1 racing wasn't a realistic proposition.

But by the time I got close to getting into F1, I wasn't quite so raw any more. By then I had already driven for Fred Opert and I was to continue doing so until I could go full time in Formula One. Fred gave me the opportunity to race all over the world. If it had wheels, I drove it. In a single year he and I did five continents in F2 and Formula Atlantic. It was the busiest year I've ever put in; I doubt any driver ever had a busier. Every other week in the United States and every other week in Europe for a whole season. I started the season in New Zealand and ended it in Argentina. There was a lot going on.

It was then that I took the decisive step. I didn't allow myself just to think about getting into F1; I decided that it was to be the next step, that it was what I intended to do. Once again, I was realistic about my chances. No use knocking on the door of one of the top teams and saying, 'Hey, what about me?' I had no money; I had to make a living. I knew my chance was to take something no one else wanted and prove what I could do, even in less favourable circumstances.

My chance came when Eddie Cheever turned down the Theodore drive. He did two races, didn't qualify and then said the car wasn't good enough for him. If it wasn't good enough for him, it was fantastic for me. At the time, I had a package: I was supposed to be going to Japan to drive a Kojima. I jumped that boat before it fell apart. The car hadn't turned a wheel, but I was the driver. Theodore came up and I leaped at it. Willie Kauhsen, who had set up the Kojima deal, was pretty upset. But I didn't believe that he'd really get the package together or that he'd succeed if he did. What's more, I didn't think it would give me a chance to stay with a team.

Theodore probably took me because when Cheever turned them down – he was a BMW F2 works driver at the time – they thought they'd better take someone who was less of a hotshot.

Youth differs from age in the sport in one other important respect: it is less heedful of the possible harm that can befall it. Youth doesn't think ahead. It has less experience of what can happen when things go wrong. It has so much to prove that it does not consider the consequences. The young lions come in and, at the end of two or three years, come out – not tame tabby cats, but vastly more experienced, secure and careful. Keke was no different.

In 1979 I blew an awful lot of tyres. I think I was the only driver in Can-Am who could so overheat his tyres that they were bound to blow. I did a lot of stupid things at that time. I knew that if I took a brand-new set of tyres I could heat them up to the point of explosion; and also that I could get one super-fast lap out of them before they blew. I had five blowouts that year.

In the next-to-last race that season, at Laguna Seca, I did a fast lap but I wasn't quite sure it was fast enough. I was perfectly conscious of what I should do. I should do a slow lap, cool the tyres off and then have another try. Not me. I'm going to go out for another quick one. On the first corner, lap 5, a front tyre blows. It was 85 per cent bound to happen. There was a 15 per cent chance it might not and I was willing to risk that to get pole position.

That Can-Am crash taught me a big lesson. I hit a bank of earth like a wall at 175 m.p.h. I had terrible concussion, broken ribs, a damaged wrist. I couldn't drive from the hotel to the race track; I had to be driven. But I raced the next day. I couldn't hold the steering wheel, so they used double-sided tape and bound my hand to the wheel. But after the warm-up I was so whacked I had to go and lie down on a bed for three hours. I took three weeks to recover. That was me, young. But I was already an old man.

Why did I do things like that? I don't know. I don't know what makes me tick. I don't know why I should enjoy a qualifying lap. It's lunacy. Or like climbing mountains. It's determination, building yourself up.

It wasn't just ambition. I'd gone to race in Can-Am because I thought I'd lost my chance in F1. I thought, Sure, one day I'll get back into F1, but I had nothing concrete going on and nobody watching I wanted to impress.

Now I think about it. I didn't then. When you're younger, you have less to lose and a lot more to gain. The truth, too, is that if you think you're going to get killed in a racing car you don't get into it in the first place. You create a mental block.

In the ten to fifteen years I've been driving racing cars I've driven more and lived more than some people who've lived a hundred years. I look back at being young and I think, If I'd stayed where I was, if I'd become a schoolteacher for instance, I would have had an infinitely less rich life. As a teacher, I would have been smaller-minded. The sport, with all its risks, has developed me as a person. I always wanted that 'something bigger'. Can you do it? That's the challenge. Maybe it's the car that lets you do certain things, but you still think it's you who's doing that corner faster than you did it on the last lap. You have something to prove to yourself. The beginning, when you're young, is to start climbing the ladder. As long as you're still climbing, you can claim you're happy.

Beginning in a sport is all about learning. The only times I have acted dangerously in my later, wiser years have been when I was up against someone who hadn't learned his trade properly, as with Andrea de Cesaris in Monaco in 1982, when I really blew my cool. It's usually when I see a race slipping away from me because of some other driver who is not significant in the race, someone who is just an obstacle, like a stone in my path.

In Rio last year I was having a long battle with Elio de Angelis when I came up against one of the RAM cars. The good old doctor: Jonathan Palmer. It was his first Grand Prix finish: great for him. But he was standing still on the track and I had one of those moments of anger.

One of the first things I learned when I came into the sport was not to be in someone's way. Do your job as well as you can but don't bother those drivers who are out there trying to win the race. I like to think I'm still very careful about that: I'm only in someone's way if it's a calculated decision. Sometimes that requires fine judgement, but lapping incidents are among the most annoying things in F1.

In qualifying, everyone takes the greatest care possible. I know that sometimes it's unavoidable that you're going to be in someone's way: your head is full of your own worries, the temperature's rising, you're looking at your gauges, checking your tyres, going slow, and someone is coming up behind you a thousand times quicker than you. It should not happen, but it sometimes does. As long as you do your best, it shouldn't worry you too much.

But there are people coming up today who don't have that attitude. They have come up so fast, their attitude isn't formed yet. They don't think that because they're getting into something big they have to learn, as I did; the ink is hardly dry on their contracts before they think of themselves as fully fledged F1 drivers.

I can remember going to Wolf in 1979 and Peter Warr telling me not to forget the opportunity I was being given. We went to Dijon and I raced against Carlos Reutemann in the Lotus and beat him square after a huge battle. It wasn't a high finish, but it was the first finish for Wolf that year and I was very pleased. I wasn't silly about it or anything, but Peter said, 'Look, don't get any ideas; we're getting somewhere but it takes two years to make a GP winner.'

Wise words.

I learned a lot from Peter because I was willing to listen and take his advice. I told him I was going to race at Le Mans. Peter said, 'Are you out of your mind? Have you ever been there?' I said, 'No, but they're offering me a lot of money.' Peter's reply was, 'Yeah, that may be, but I've been there with Lotus, and if I were you I wouldn't go there.' I asked him why, and he answered, 'There are sixty or more drivers there, and only about fifteen of them are true professionals. The rest keep bars or run companies or whatever. Racing at 350 k.p.h. in the rain against amateurs can't be the hobby you're looking for.'

I didn't go; I haven't been since and I probably never will. As I say, you're in this business to learn from those who know more than you do, and if you disregard their advice then you're just a fool. A lot of the young ones today haven't learned to listen to their elders.

Of course, so much depends on how you start. If you start in the way I started, you learn very little. I started with a poor team. If you start with a good team, you can't help learning.

When I returned to F1 in 1979 with Peter Warr I began learning. Peter had the experience; good teams embody experience. They've had major drivers, they've had the best engineers, they've been at it a long time; they have solid support; they've thought out all the problems of the sport. With Peter I could take a different attitude than with Teddy Yip and Sid Taylor. I was no longer the guy who knew it all. I don't think I ever really was, but when you're with people who know even less than you do, it's hard not to be impatient. Generally, the attitude of being a know-all isn't going to get you very far, in F1 or anywhere else in motor sport or in life.

I would contrast Alain Prost and Andrea de Cesaris on that score. Prost was a good learner from the start. He did a year at McLaren, who have a long history in the sport, and then moved to Renault. Big teams. Good places to learn. Andrea, who is the youngest driver in F1, thinks he knows it all; he carried that attitude with him to McLaren. Misfortune may have taught him a lot, but he still has a way to go.

In 1983 we started driving turbos. I knew nothing whatever about driving a turbo car. I had to learn a whole new technique of driving: what makes it go, how to make it last. The world of the turbos is full of secrets. Niki said the same thing: that the reason Prost was quicker than he this past year was that Prost had been driving turbos for three years longer than he had. Niki wasn't too proud to admit he was still learning.

You can tell the drivers who learn from those who don't. Prost and Piquet are both good finishers, even if this year Nelson had an unusual number of engine blow-ups, which were no fault of his own. Cheever and Patrese are not good finishers. They weren't good finishers at Renault or at Brabham, so it can't be just the Alfa that's wrong. They must be mistreating their engine somehow; if not, why does Piquet's engine hold up and Patrese's not? Why does Prost finish and not Cheever?

The young sometimes ignore the rest of the world, as though it did not exist. They don't watch how others do things; they don't listen when engineers and team managers talk to them. They have supreme confidence in their own abilities. That's a good thing. You can't race without it. But your self-confidence shouldn't be so great that it stops you from learning. The younger you are, the more you should be keeping your eyes and ears open. Out there, there is always someone who is thinking and driving better than you are. There is always something that someone else does better than you do.

It's not a question of modelling yourself on someone else. You can't really do that in motor racing because drivers are so different – in style, in attitude, in approach – from each other. But you can be aware of someone else's mental attitude, of how he approaches a problem and the sport in general. I watch videos of motor races as entertainment; but I also try to understand why at a given point so-and-so did this or that.

It was fantastic being young. It's also good being less young. There are different problems at different ages. Life changes, and that is good. I've always liked change. There may come a time when I like change less, a time when I want to stand still. I'll try that too. After my last race.

2

From Bikes to Karts

Keke inherited his father's kart, an American Dart with a 100-cc Parilla air-turbine-cooled engine. The first Rosberg victory was in 1965 in Kouvola. At seventeen he bought his own kart and signed up for nineteen races. He won the Finnish and Nordic championships and was selected for the Finnish team. Lasse Rosberg, ever involved, was mechanic and confidant. That summer Keke worked in Sweden in a garage, learning his trade. Scampering around the garage was a little kid, Stefan Johansson. 1967 brought another Finnish championship and the following year, despite his baccalaureate exams, Keke travelled all over Central Europe karting.

In the autumn of 1968 he did his military service; it was not a serious impediment to his karting. He raced in Copenhagen, flew back to Reserve Officers School while the karts travelled to Germany, and rejoined them in Fulda; afterwards he flew back to his barracks. His national service over, Keke competed full time. Without sponsorship, the financial burden – on both Keke and his father – was great. There was no money for karts, least of all for Finns. He also twice failed his exams. He married for the first time and settled in Helsinki, working for a computer firm.

Karting

Karting for me was the good old days. It's the best possible training there is: you get a feel for the road, for the machinery, and it's intimate in scale. It's not by chance that many F1 drivers started in karts.

The truth is, however, that my father and I did everything arse backwards in those days! Imagine the two of us: a schoolboy and a veterinarian, neither of them with a clue about the mechanical or technical aspects of the sport. I knew nothing about the subtleties of driving and I think the pair of us knew even less about organization.

It cost us both a lot of money. When I look back on those days, I'm still surprised at the results we managed to get from such trifling means. If we had spent the same money each year with specialists and if there had been any sponsors about, we might have had far better results. But those were really good times, and being close to my father and making friends who remain my friends are only some of the good things about that period. My last years in karting were already financed by business, in this case my own motor racing business: buy karts and engines from an expert, buy from Rosberg.

Money

The modern driver is very concerned with money. Back in the so-called good old days so celebrated by the nostalgic, a driver spent his own money to race. He might win back a bit, but on the whole he was on the debit side. Then came the notion of the 'professional' sportsman. From sport to sport it swept like wildfire, bringing into what had started as competition between individuals a whole new race of middle men: money brokers, managers and commercial exploiters.

Motor racing was a natural field. It was international, it was at the time, relatively glamorous, it was high tech, it was risky, and it was very expensive to stage. What more natural than that the driver, who was the visible heart of the show, should seek to advertise himself, support himself and thus help defray some of the costs of his participation? And if the driver, why not the team?

The result was an instant escalation of the costs of the sport. If one could run a racing team in the fifties for $100,000, by the sixties the sum had risen to double that. With the advent of sponsorship, the sport was economically unleashed. By the mid-seventies the figure had passed $1 million. Today, a competitive team needs to pull in some $7–$8 million just to function.

Consciousness of money has made the drivers into something more than merely professional sportsmen. They are now the creatures of accountants and tax lawyers; they live in exotic, tax-free venues; they invest their earnings; they maximize their commercial possibilities. The beginnings may be hard, but at the peak of the sport the driver may earn – in what is *acknowledgedly a short and perilous decade in the sport – a very great deal of money, somewhere between half a million dollars a year for the lesser sort, to well over $2 million for those at the top.*

But between drivers there remains a great financial gap. There are those who are smart with their money and those who are less smart. And, of course, there are those who make a lot and those who not only don't make much but sometimes – more often than is supposed – actually shell out money in order to race and to prove their own worth, something very few pay-as-you-drive racers have ever done.

Keke has always admitted that his interest in racing was twofold: what started as a pure desire to compete extended to cover all the marketing aspects of the sport. The base remained the same, but the overall picture became much larger. Very few drivers have had precisely the same attitude towards the business side of the sport as Keke has: if business is part of sport, then business too, in and of itself, is of interest.

Exactly how the two subjects are intertwined for a driver is something most people who follow the sport do not know.

I left karting because of money. It was and always has been my dream to be able to retire from the sport at thirty-five, though it does not look at though I'm actually going to do that. Back in those days I could have retired on £100,000 and lived on the interest quite happily. That was once my goal. But one's goals change, and once I got into the sport at a more advanced level it was only natural that I should think higher.

My present goals are not that money-oriented. But to have goals, whether in business or in motor racing, is important. They are the challenge. Goals that are set by myself for myself. I have no doubt about it. I will have that sum. It's part of my overall plan in motor racing and in business in general.

There is always something that makes a man tick. In my case it is also financial independence. I probably have enough right now to be financially independent, but I couldn't live as I want to live, I couldn't live at the same standard. That doesn't mean that I could not live happily, but I still have some unfulfilled ambitions.

Among those unfulfilled ambitions is my racing. I still like it and I still want to go racing. Therefore, why quit? I want to maximize a given opportunity. Motor racing is that opportunity; it would be foolish to throw away something for which I have been working ten long, hard years. When I talk about opportunity, I mean in part financial opportunity. The other part lies in the sport itself. I have set myself certain goals and I still have not attained them.

I've won a few Grands Prix, I've won the world championship, I've won at Monaco, which is something special. But I want to win the championship again, I want to win more races. I can't explain why I want to. It is just important to me.

Winning the championship is, of course, more than a sporting coup. It brings you more than celebrity. It also brings in the money to achieve your other aims. When you win it, when you win anything, you have to maximize the benefits of what you have earned the hard way. You can't do that simply by saying, 'Hey I'm champion', and then going to sleep. I work much harder in the off season than I work during the championship itself.

My rise in the sport and my championship came too quickly. I was not properly tooled up to take advantage of what I had achieved. In business terms, I did not have the time or the resources to follow it up properly. My businesses weren't ready for it. They lagged behind. I had just one win, one championship and one season on which to build. It takes more time than that to build a business to the level to take advantage of being champion. I came from nowhere. Now I am prepared to take advantage of what I can still do in the future.

There is a lot of learning to do. I learned from other drivers. It wasn't hard to see that, in terms of self-exploitation, Niki was doing everything right and Nelson was doing everything wrong. That is not a moral criticism or any kind of criticism. If I wanted to go on racing for another fifteen years, as I suspect Nelson does, if that was all that interested me, I would do exactly as Nelson does: enjoy my racing, enjoy my free time and pay no attention to the money aspects, and even Nelson has to fight very hard to maintain his privacy and his independence. There is no easy way. But, like Niki, I have other interests. I don't want to race cars for the rest of my life. Perhaps if all the races were in my back garden, I wouldn't stop. But I wasn't born to live in aeroplanes and hotels. Some people are born to live like gypsies; not I.

So you have to exploit what you've got now. How do you do that? By working as hard as you can with the public. The public is your bread and butter. They want to see you, they want to be connected with you,. As a world champion you have a significant income, but it is up to you to build on that base. As I said, I came to my championship too quickly. There was a gap between my being champion and the public's perception of that fact. By working with the public, by making connections, by appearances, by endorsements, by all the other means of publicity, my job is to make the world aware of who is world champion: to make them aware of me as a driver, to make them aware of me as a personality.

It is hard work. It means saying yes whenever you're asked to do something. But before you can do that, you have to create an organization which can cope with the flow of demands, which can schedule those demands, which can set fees. Now I have such an organization. It makes decisions for me. The world at large can't reach me when it wants to. My manager, Ortwin Podlech, handles all the decisions for me. He has my full trust and I generally do what he says.

The money aspect is only part of it. If you are asked to appear on television, it isn't necessarily the fee you get for appearing that counts, it's the exposure you will get from that experience. That exposure will lead to other things. The same is true of columns in newspapers and magazines, books, personal appearances and so on.

Naturally enough, there is a set of fixed fees for all these activities, just as there is for whatever I do. There is a fixed fee for driving, there is a fixed fee for wearing a Marlboro badge on my overalls. The fees vary according to place and importance, just as the location of a sponsor's badge on my overalls or my helmet is part of the price. How visible is it? How often will it be seen on television or in photographs? And, of course, how often will it be seen on the podium! It's not for nothing that Parmalat, Goodyear, Michelin and so on hire people to make sure that drivers wear their hats – sometimes several in sequence – on the podium. You can be sure that the shot of a driver holding a wreath and a bottle of champagne (that too is paid for) will be seen in every part of the world, in every imaginable medium.

Thus there is a price list for everything. The price rises and falls according to how well you are doing, how famous you are or how famous you can make yourself. In some circumstances you reduce the fee. If you stay with a certain company for a long time and they support you through thick and thin, you can let them have you for less. You know the people, you get along. It saves time and hassle not to be too exacting, not try always to hustle for the maximum. Loyalty counts for something in business. So does reasonableness.

Television, radio, newspapers and magazines are in a different category. They are the sources of your celebrity and you have to know how to cope with them; you have to know what is going to advance your cause. They need you and you need them. The result is a trade-off. You do most of that for free. The pennies will fall somewhere farther down the line.

A world championship requires a very special form of exploitation. You know you have to make your jackpot right then and there. No one can guarantee that you're going to be sitting pretty the next year. The close season of your championship does not last for ever. You have a few months in which to maximize your profit; after that, business slows down. Roughly speaking, you could say that you keep your championship price tag but you get fewer takers. There are always plenty of opportunities to keep a world champion busy. When business slows down, then you have to go out and look for more.

Between October and Christmas it's pretty hectic. There are pictures, photography sessions, autograph sessions, trade shows, fashion pictures, magazine features, racing car exhibitions. The list is as unending as ingenuity itself. Basically, the champion works on a good hourly rate. For X amount of dollars he will turn up in place and do whatever is required of him: meet customers, appear in trade shows, shake hands, smile, be nice to VIPs, hold a glass of beer in his hand, smoke Brand Z. Like the media, it's a two-way street. You are serving someone else's interests. They are making something out of it; you are making something out of it. But, beyond that, you are showing yourself to the public, you are cultivating your fame. The more

34

people see you, the happier the major sponsors are. The more people read about you, the happier they are.

They are making something out of it: I am making something out of it. It's a big opportunity, I learn a hell of a lot. You meet top people in all sorts of trades. These people can always be useful and if you use your brains, you can always learn something. After winning the championship, I had a few days off, and then I started work. That meant taking up all the offers that had come in during the year. They come in all the time, not only on the Monday after the last race, but you don't always have the time available to accept some of them. We'd been raising the price slowly throughout the year as I was in contention. That's the smart way to do it. You can't just jump your fee by a factor of ten because you're champion. If you know what's coming, you build up your reputation slowly and carefully; the reputation grows throughout the season. At the end you should be able to take advantage of it. I didn't actually close the gap between reputation and fee until late in the winter. By that time I was totally exhausted. It's hard, when it's all new to you and you know you have to make hay while the sun shines, to say no to anything that seems likely to enhance your long-term aims.

As for the amount of money a champion can make out of his success, that is a deep, dark secret. There is no price published; the activities are too many, the contracts too complex, for anyone to know the real answer. Drivers are by habit very secretive about money; they're suspicious of each other and compete over money exactly as they do over cars and in a race.

But the fees are set on all sorts of different bases. There are drivers who want to work and make money that way – like myself. But when you come to the fees for driving a car, the retainers paid to each driver, that is a jungle. It's a highly specialized field. There are those who set their fees low because they want to stay in the sport; there are those who set their fees high because they don't want to join a particular team; but they will if their fee is met. The variations are endless.

Basically the fee is set because you know your profession and the market. The point is to know your value. Your value as a driver and your value to a particular team. It's the same with the commercial work. The price is set by the time it takes. If you do a session next door to your home, an hour is an hour; if you have to go to Zürich or Stockholm, an hour's work means a day's disruption. But you balance that against other things you might be able to develop in the same place. I do a lot of things that don't make money directly but take time none the less. An ad agency charges their time on a budget; my people do the same with my time.

I don't like to be pressed on this subject! I'm as secretive as the next man.

Making money is an instinct. You've got it or you haven't. You are a salable commodity or you aren't. I think I'm a marketable commodity. Not only because my championship and all my years in different forms of racing have made me well known, and not only because I've consistently up-graded my image, but for all sorts of other reasons, not least of which are my languages. I can work anywhere. Scandinavia isn't my sole market. Obviously Finland is important; there are a lot of international companies based in Finland. For instance, the state oil corporation, NESTE, is a big trading company. When I won the championship, they worked fantastically well for me, and I for them. The title of the advertisement was 'The Formula of becoming Number One'. They listed the relevant details of the company and of my career: both born the same year. That was a smart ad. Finland is a very advanced country for advertising, like the United States.

I love marketing. I love people who are creative in business. If you ask me where this love comes from, I have no ready answer. Perhaps I was born with it. Perhaps it was born from my youthful desire to retire at thirty-five. My father was certainly not commercial when he was working; if he had been, perhaps he would have gone on racing. But, for me, being successful in business is as much a pleasure as being successful in racing. I get the same thing out of each: a feeling that I am making the most out of my opportunities.

3

From Karting to FVee 1300

Success in karts: 1968, second in the Finnish championship; 1970, Finnish champion, fifth in the world championship; 1971, second in the Finnish championship. Keke was still an amateur. He wanted to move upwards. It was the autumn of 1971 and his family was against it; he had no private money behind him and not that many prospects. None the less, he bought a Veemax and in April 1972 was fourth against the best in FVee 1300.

Already he was smart enough to know local reputations don't count for much. And to know his own mind. His career was formed in his head. In the summer of 1972 he headed south and toured in both karting and FVee: Liedolsheim, the Lido of Jesolo, Salzburg, Zeltweg, Hockenheim. The travels had begun; the circuits that were going to be his took on reality. But money was a problem: his very small-time sponsor failed to pay the bills. That meant no tyres, no engine rebuilds. It didn't help that he had two accidents.

For 1973 he got right down to business. Commerce entered. Sunoco, the Viking Line, Monza and a Finnish sporting paper were among his first sponsors. He joined the Colt Racing Team. The results, in a Hansen MkIVB that belonged to the outgoing Swedish champion Tommy Brorsson, were impressive: nineteen races, fifteen wins, two second places, two retirements. One of the victories was at the Nürburg-ring. The old one. He was European champion.

The years in FVee 1300, especially the second, were invaluable. They taught me that racing is just not taking the wheel but also preparing the engines, looking after the public relations and making the necessary contacts. It was there that I learned how to be a professional. I learned languages and got away from the rather narrow Finnish background in which I had grown up. Those years gave me self-confidence, a belief in my own capacities as a driver. I still had no grand design, but I was on my way. I was at the bottom of the ladder, but I had made a name for myself. That was at least as important as the trophies I won. It was a launching platform.

Naturals

For any driver the most important thing by far is that he should have a natural feeling for the car. He doesn't have to be a flawless athlete in the sense that all his movements are coordinated and beautiful, but he must have a good relationship between his arms and legs, between his head and his eyes, between his brain and his body. Not everyone has the required degree of control. Co-ordination is part of the driver's natural feeling.

Everything in a racing car happens exceedingly quickly; all the movements you make, like the decisions you take, are almost automatic: gear-changes, turns, feeding in power, lifting off, accelerating. For none of these do you have any time to think. Questions run through your mind all the time: should I give it more power? Shall I open up the throttle? Sometimes you actually think out what you should do and still it doesn't happen. You say, faster; but to go faster you should have pushed your foot deeper. You come to the same place on the next lap and again your foot still doesn't go deep enough. Your head tells you you ought to do it, you must do it, but your foot either can't or won't. And sometimes it's the other way around: your foot does it when your head says it shouldn't.

Without that coordination, without that natural feeling, no one could possibly drive a racing car. Every driver starts with it. Perhaps some have it more than others. If you ask how much coordination is required, the answer is 100 per cent.

Nor is it possible to differentiate between coordination and reflex. When you've performed these actions as often and for as long as I have, they become automatic. It is as natural to do them as it is to blink. And they are not something you learn; at least, not in my case. I found them easy from the start. Good coordination is something you ought to have before you even begin to drive fast. On the road you often see people who are not co-ordinated; they are not at ease with their cars. It is like looking at someone who is struggling against the water instead of using it to keep himself afloat. I've never seen anyone uncoordinated in a racing car. I've seen drivers who don't look coordinated out of their cars, drivers who look strong rather than graceful, but once in their cars they're completely smooth and at ease.

I may be overdoing the instinctive and 'natural' aspects of driving. A lot of that 'natural' feeling comes from practice, from making the same motions over and over again during years and years of driving. Still, I suspect that it is easier for some than for others.

Similarly, there are those whom the press and others describe as 'smooth' drivers. It's not something I think about at all: being smooth. I drive the way I feel. I drive naturally, in accordance with my temperament, and until someone proves to me that's wrong, that's the way I shall continue to drive.

I lost one possible drive because I wasn't what some people call smooth. In this case the critic was Jackie Stewart. Jackie said, 'This guy is not smooth, he'll never be able to drive a racing car.' He has yet to prove me wrong.

When I look at top drivers, I can think of Niki and Nelson who drive 'smoothly' – when their cars and the conditions are right. I've also seen them struggling against cars that weren't handling smoothly. Then they look less smooth. But Villeneuve was never smooth; he was pretty quick. The same was true of Ronnie Peterson, who was as quick as hell. Alan Jones was no smoothie. Different people do different things in different ways. Each man's handwriting is different and the way each man handles a car is different. Each driver is different and often the cars are different.

When you see another driver on the track ahead of you, you can't exactly identify him by the way he is driving, but when you're up with him and racing him, then his style emerges, his driving follows a pattern which is natural to him. He has his own way of thinking, his own way of driving, just as he has his own character and his own way of talking. You don't say to yourself, that's Tambay or that's Prost; you can't predict entirely what he is going to do. But you do have a certain picture of him; you have a 'feel' for him.

4

From Amateur to Professional

In 1974, to climb up the next rung of the ladder, Keke had a number of choices. F3 had its prestige, especially in England. The problem was money. For Super Vee, FVee 1600, he already had the contacts. And then there was F2 beckoning.

Kurt Bergman of the Kaimann team offered Keke a contract for 1974. Keke was part of a noble lineage: Jochen Rindt, Dieter Quester, Niki Lauda and Jochen Mass all raced for Bergman. The question had become: did Keke have enough talent to survive as a pro, to earn his living from the sport? It seemed there was no way he could keep both job and his sport. But his employer, Sperry Rand Univac, gave him a year off for racing.

He set himself up in a caravan at Zell am See in Austria where, many years later, he was to buy a house. The season began in April at the Nürburgring. Disappointment. Retirements and fourth and fifth places. Not until July did he win, on the team's home circuit in Zeltweg. Another triumph at Silverstone made him think he could still finish third in the championship. It worked out, although he somersaulted at Hockenheim on 25 September the last race of the series. The record remained good: twenty-one races, fourteen places, including seven wins, (two of them in FVee): third in the VW Gold Cup and second in the Castrol GTX Trophy.

The balance sheet of my first year as a professional remains satisfactory. Perhaps I shouldn't have been so pleased with myself; after all, only winning counts. But I had set myself certain goals for the season and I went beyond them in each case. For instance, I got an offer to race in F5000 from McKechnie Racing. That meant I was already considered a pro, someone who could go higher. At the end of the year the future looked more promising.

Keke was at last sure he could earn his living from the sport. However, while Kaimann offered cars and engines, they offered no salary. That was one problem. Second, the Bergman engine left Keke unconvinced. Third, was not a second year in Super Vee a step backwards, or standing still? Money, money, always money; every team said, 'How much money can you bring?'

Salvation came from the rag trade – from Uwe and Boss, the German clothing giant, later a big sponsor in Formula One – and from a Finnish motoring magazine and Kamei, which makes auto accessories. The team consisted of Keke, Prince Ludwig of Bavaria, Thomas Teves and Uwe Jurdens. The manager was Ortwin Podlech, who was to become Keke's manager and confidant. Finally, the engines came from Heidegger.

The 1975 season began brilliantly: three victories in three races – the Nürburgring in a snowstorm, Aspern near Vienna, and Hockenheim, but the final results were less good than Keke expected: a lot of engine failures and fifth in the main competition, the VW Gold Cup, but first in the Castrol GTX Trophy, the German Super Vee championship and second in the Solex Cup. Twenty-one races, fifteen results, nine victories in the various categories.

A great start to the season and then pfft! Two seasons in Super Vee is enough. With a third one stops growing. What I had to do next was concentrate on using my reputation and all the contacts I'd made to change formulas. My aim was F2, but first I had to get a foot in the door.

At the end of the season, Fred Opert, the American agent for Chevron, met in earlier days, reappeared in Keke's life. Keke raced a Supernova at Watkins Glen and was placed sixth amongst the best Americans. An important friendship was renewed.

Transitions

I never asked myself whether I was good enough to keep going up the formulas or to get to F1, to the top. I went into racing to drive FVee cars. When I did that, I realized I was bored with my job in computers. I wasn't very good at it and it was taking too much of the time I wanted to give to racing.

From that it was just a step to giving up the job. With prudence, of course. Having taken a year's leave, I realized I could make a living racing, so at the end of 1974 I went back to my employer and said, 'I'm not coming back.' I did another year of Super Vee. Then I got fed up with that.

You don't know how or why you make the leap from one category to another. It's a matter of opportunity and of working to a long-range goal. At the beginning, it was just instinct. I knew I would never get anywhere if I wasn't *known*. No one is going to ask you to drive for him if he doesn't know you exist. Even at the lowest levels of racing, even in Formula Vee, I was conscious that it was important to get a good press.

The relationship between driver and the press is symbiotic. The journalist exists because the sport exists, and drivers, human copy, are what makes good ink. In the same way, drivers need the press, radio, television, exposure. Not only do they need it, they often enjoy it. The sport is enough of a family for the press to feel part of it. And why not? They share the same lives, the same venues, the same travel, the same hotels and, often, the same ideals. Thus the writer uses the driver and the driver uses the writer. Even if this were not instinctive, the driver's team and the sponsors insist on it. Team and driver combine to create occasions for photographs and articles.

In general, Keke has had a poor press since he came into F1. And when he became world champion he got an even poorer press. This was not because he lacked affability, or willingness, or a sense of self-interest, but largely because the Williams team had a distinctly ambivalent attitude towards the press. Frank Williams himself had suffered from harsh things said about him in his earlier days in the sport; he had been ill-considered, neglected and often reviled. Being the sort of obsessive, introverted, fanatically disciplined man he is, it became a matter of habit with him to break the conventional links between press and driver and team. A fierce nationalist, shy and afraid of being misunderstood, he put up a sign in his motor-home window that said 'English press welcome'. The English press operated by his rules, in a way that he understood; from them he expected, and largely got, sympathy and respect. From the French, the Italians and others, not unnaturally, he got neglect.

Thus the notion grew up that Keke was an outsider, a loner, a man who would not talk to the press. The truth is quite other. There is a part of the press that is opinionated, that is not objective, that has private axes to grind. There are English journalists who rubbish Renault; there are French journalists who worship only Lotus. Keke and Frank Williams had no natural constituency in the world press; and despite Keke's efforts, the ever-present smile, the politeness, the attention paid to sponsors, what Williams did directly affected Keke.

Losses

Everyone knows what a driver gains from being in F1: he is promoted to the top of his profession; in most cases he makes good money; he acquires certain worldly goods – if at the top, big cars, the odd yacht, a private plane, all the tools and trappings of the trade – a form of instant fame, a recognition factor, a way of jumping through the world's queues; a façade of adventure and travel, elegant women, instant access to the beau monde. *What few people bother to think about are the corresponding losses. What is it, beyond the physical stress, the constant danger, the enforced servitude, the harassments of the trade – and its insecurity – that a driver loses?*

What you lose is very much defined by what you have or would like to have. It's very different from driver to driver. Some come in who are party types, skiing types; obviously that goes out the window. F1 has no room for parties that last much beyond ten at night. On the other hand, if you had been a nine-to-five man, then I suppose you've gained a good deal. But most of us come into racing without really well-established habits, so what we do in F1 very much becomes a habit.

The chief loss, clearly, is a loss of normalcy. F1 is not a normal life; you can't expect to lead a normal, steady life in F1. The total commitment you have to make to the sport if you want to be successful puts a lot of strain on a normal family life, for instance; if you marry, you must expect a certain amount of strain. That is, you cannot put into marriage and family life the commitment that you might like to. That is a different kind of commitment. Like friends, wives tend to suffer from neglect.

I first married in my early days. It would be too easy to say that that marriage fell apart because of my racing. There was a lack of understanding on her part, yes; but certainly my racing played a major part in undoing our marriage. I was working night and day to get what I wanted. She wasn't prepared to live with a man who had to live like that. She felt she wasn't getting from marriage what she wanted. Also, her goals in life were very different from mine.

It is not acceptable in today's liberated climate to say this, but a woman who marries a racing driver in a certain sense has to live *for* him. Her only other choice is to live a life for herself, which can lead to trouble. I've seen it work both ways and I've seen it fail both ways. I've also seen marriages where it's impossible to tell which is more important, the wife or the racing. I think it best to keep everyone out of it when I'm working.

That doesn't mean to say that a wife shouldn't be around. Frankly, I love to have Sina there when I race. Her presence should make it easier for me to relax in the evenings when the job is done: the only trouble is I don't get any time to relax in the evenings because I'm working with my sponsors nine tenths of the time. But it's better if she's there. There was a time when I wasn't so busy, when I wasn't married. And I suppose I played around. Now I've grown up: I'm married again and I don't have the urge to go out and play around.

If you're hunting women, being a driver helps, sure – it's a glamorous job, seen from the outside – but it depends on whether you really need that advantage to attract a woman, if all you want out of women is what you can get by using your position. As always between the sexes, it depends what you're looking for. I've gone through that period, too.

I'm basically a discreet person, but I've always lived with a woman. They have never been an interference in my professional life, though I can understand how certain women might be. That's quite simple: if your woman is an impediment to your reaching your goals, your choice is clear: it's the woman or the goals. For me, that would be a very simple decision.

The glamour of racing is pretty fictitious anyway. A woman who sets her cap at a man because he is a racing driver quickly finds out how unglamorous the profession is; and if she wants him because he has money, then that's no different from any other job. Ten or more years ago driving was probably one hell of a way to live. It was, they tell me, a world full of characters. Not now. If you take your job seriously, there's precious little time for anything else, but plenty of character-*building*.

I used to burn the candle at both ends. Not any more. I'm too busy and too dedicated. It's not in my system now and I don't miss it. Nor do I have any regrets that I once lived that way. Now I have neither the need nor the desire, but I suppose if I had either I wouldn't hesitate.

What's called 'settling down' is an iffy proposition. I like the idea and I don't. The older you get, the more cautious you get. If you have children, then you should get married and settle down; if you don't have children, there's no need to get married. That doesn't mean it's a bad idea to do so. I don't find it difficult to imagine having children. That is one of life's pleasures; it is perhaps one of the things you lose in the sport, though there's no real reason why that should be so. Having children makes life that much more difficult, but life is not easy anyway. You would want to spend more time with your family and that would alter the rhythm of your life. Gilles Villeneuve had kids; it didn't bother him. Prost has kids; it doesn't change his professional life. My wife is pregnant and I can hardly wait.

Some people say you get more cautious when you drive if you have kids, but nobody could be more cautious than I am now anyway. So it's not going to make any difference to me. It may alter more personal values, but not my professional life. It probably has something to do with age. Maybe you don't want to miss out on so much any more; you start to want to do other things. But when that happens, when you no longer want to give 100 per cent or you no longer can, that's the time to quit.

On the subject of loss, I can remember Alan Jones saying that no driver could really give 100 per cent twice to racing, and that was why he did not want to come back after retiring. His decision had to do with wanting to be with his family. Lauda is proof to the contrary. Other champions, both in motor racing and in other sports, have lost more by quitting racing than they might have lost by staying in the sport. There is a going-to-seed which accompanies giving up something that has been so much a part of one's life. Perhaps life itself loses a little of its savour. Again, Lauda is proof to the contrary. So is Jackie Stewart. Let's say that those who have enough going for them outside the sport while they're in the sport are also those who can survive outside the sport without a sense of loss.

Marriage

Keke has been married twice: once at the time when he failed his exams and got his first job in computing; the second time on the island of Mauritius after the 1983 season, to Gesine Dengel, known universally as Sina, a tall, refined blonde a year or two older than Keke. Rather than being his foil, Sina seems to be very much an amalgam of his qualities: she has a degree of cool common sense, practicality, a love of home and animals, of the sun and relaxation. Both have seen hard times, Keke in one of the hardest of sporting professions, and Sina emotionally and personally. Together they offer each other mutual support and intimacy in a world of competition and publicity. But the adaptation of any wife to the milieu is not always easy. From the outside, it seems hard on the woman. Not just because of the travelling and the exigencies of her husband's trade, but because there is so little time for a personal life and because he has so many commitments that she is required to subordinate her own life to his. And then there is the solitude, the daily presence of risk, the very small social world, the same losses a driver feels when he signs on: the loss of friends, native habitat, roots, privacy . . .

Marriage is not harder for the driver than for any other man, only different in that the life itself is special. I recognize the disadvantages, the chief of which is the endless travelling, the endless uprooting, the packing, the remembering, the never being in one place long enough.

Too much is made of the risks all drivers take and their effect on our wives. I don't think anyone close to a driver thinks about the risks in the same way an outsider does. They don't think about the risks consciously; they probably feel just a generalized, subconscious anxiety.

We are very conscious about doing things together, Sina and I. Sometimes I'll go somewhere Sina doesn't want to visit. She doesn't like Japan, for example, mainly because it's cold and she loves the heat. Otherwise, at least for the present, she loves travelling. She has friends nearly everywhere, so she gets along wherever we are. I don't think she feels lonely.

The adaptation must in part rest on the interest your wife takes in your profession, on what you do for a hundred days a year, which is drive a car professionally, and on what you do for the rest of the time, which is business. If your wife isn't interested,

then her life is going to be a lot harder than if she is. Being
interested gives a wife understanding. The sport Sina obviously
lives through me. So far, she hasn't seen that much: one season.
We talk a lot about my racing. Not necessarily about the details.
We tend to talk more about my feelings, and hers, inside the
sport. She has a certain technical interest, but what she wants to
know is how things are going: was it good or bad on a particular
day? What are the problems?

For me, to have Sina around is to have my private life with me
wherever I go. When I close the door of my hotel room, I am in
another world, a more human world. Life wasn't that impossible
before I got married; but if life had been perfect, then I wouldn't
have thought it a good idea to marry. And the previous women
can't have been perfect either, or I would have got married
before. If I'd found someone who could get along with my difficult temperament before now, I wouldn't have waited until I
was thirty-five to marry again. It wasn't that I wasn't ready for
marriage; I didn't want a marriage that wouldn't be exactly
right.

I place a huge value on my private life, and the harder I work,
the greater the need I have for a private life. If anything,
marriage has made me an even more private person than before.
Marriage is a stabilizing influence; it makes you more consistent;
it eases your relations with the world outside.

I've always had long-standing relationships with women. But
when you reach thirty-five you think more deeply; you think
very differently from the way you thought when you were
younger. If I had to define the difference between now and then,
I'd say that back in my early days I was too busy to think much
about a fulfilling private life. I am no longer under the same kind
of pressure as when I was starting out, when my business affairs
were not so well ordered. Having them in decent shape leaves me
more time to concentrate on my main work, which is driving,
and on my private life, which I'd neglected before.

It is also time to decide where to live. I seem always to have
lived in foreign countries. That in itself creates work. I have
never had a steady home; there's always been something going
on. Now I hope to simplify life. Currently, we live in Ibiza – when
we are there. With Williams, it was very important for me to be

47

in England. But today it might be better to go back to Monaco and live in an apartment instead of a house. We wouldn't have to look after the garden, the gardener and everything else. I don't know about Ibiza. We love the sun and we love our house there, but both of us probably still need a little civilization every now and then. If we stayed on in Ibiza, I'd become an island person. Maybe a fisherman. Yet I feel the need for balance.

There's nothing wrong with England, but it creates too much work. Also, Sina's English is not all that hot yet; she's much more at home in French. But I love England. England is the freest, most civilized country in Europe. You can be an individual in England. I like the English, too. I don't sit down and think what I like about them; I just like them. I have friends in England and I'd like to have them around and talk to them: if I had the time.

From the team's point of view, my getting married probably didn't add to the value of Frank's investment. If you want glamour and publicity, a driver in a disco is worth twice as much as a happily married man. The media are always complaining that we drivers are an unglamorous lot these days. But they live by a double standard. If they see a driver getting off a plane drunk, they say, 'How disgusting!' If nothing happens, they say we're a dull lot and why don't we give them something to write about. I'm not here to please everybody; it can't be done anyway. Frank sent a very nice telex for the wedding; only he and Ortwin, outside the families, knew about it in advance.

On the whole, team managers don't worry much about the private lives of their drivers. Before me, Frank's number one driver was Alan Jones: not a man you could accuse of an excess of sobriety and calm. But Frank is also a very moral man. For instance, he objects to my smoking so much. If Frank had known how much I smoked, he probably wouldn't have hired me. It was Charlie Crichton-Stuart, the man who brought the team its sponsorship and whose job it was to keep sonsors happy, who told me not to smoke while my contract was being negotiated with Frank, Charlie being the only man besides myself who smokes on a tennis court! Then, as soon as Frank had agreed, I lit up. Charlie has always been the intermediary: he did for me what he did for Alan. He's the most optimistic man on earth and allows people to be just what they are, which is a gift, just as Charlie being just Charlie is a gift. He's the one who keeps the morale up; unfortunately, he left with Tag; we missed him in 1984, we missed them both. Had he been around, the edges wouldn't have got so frayed.

5

From Super Vee to F2

*In 1976 Jörg Obermoser moved up to F2 and signed Keke. The new car
was called a Toj; it was sponsored by Warsteiner and was the first new
German F2 car in five years. From the first tests at Hockenheim, Keke
felt at home. Five F1 drivers were there, including Hans Stuck. Keke
was sixteenth on the grid, but in the next race failed to qualify. Obermoser thought he might have a dud and brought in Rolf Stommelen to test;
both drivers obtained the same times. From that point matters improved—
although at Hockenheim in June Keke's seat gave way under him during
the race.*

My backside was on fire! The worst was that, as the race wore
on, I slipped farther and farther down in the cockpit until
finally I could hardly see a thing. Towards the end I had to slow
down in order not to be thrown out of the car on the corners
and sometimes I couldn't even reach the pedals.

*At the end of the season, Keke was tenth in the championship. A new team
with a new driver, he acknowledges, couldn't have hoped to do much better.
In the process, he had matured.*

Formula Two is a place for professionals. There is no opening
for amateurs. I started out thinking I could make up for the
defects of the car by sheer willpower; it spoiled my style,
though I made my mark doing so. I was not sure, however, that
I could last long enough for the team to be successful; but one
thing remained clear: I had never yet paid to drive and I had no
intention of doing so. In the first place, I had neither the
means nor the intention and in the second, I think drivers
should be chosen on merit and not for the cash in their
pockets.

It is a profession in which one is always an apprentice. There's no end to what one has to learn, and when for a moment you think you know your trade, along comes a Stuck to slide impeccably through the Ostkurve at Hockenheim and take 100 metres off you; then you know how little you know and how far you are from being a real professional.

Keke's balance for his first season in F2 was fourteen races, one win, two seconds, a fourth and a fifth, plus five retirements.

Frustration

The images we have of the sport are of triumph. Our eyes, our minds, the press and, above all, the television camera focus on winners. The other side of the sport is virtually forgotten or overlooked: that for every minute of glory, there are months and years of sheer frustration; that for every sure, confident, successful lap, there are dozens that for the driver are like butting up against a brick wall.

There is no sport like F1 for frustration. There are moments of joy, but 75 per cent of the time there is frustration. The balance would be 75 per cent frustration, 15 per cent with no feelings at all, and the rest is probably joy. The joy you can obtain from even the most minor trifles. Winning a race, sure; but also testing or qualifying or doing just one small thing right.

It's all down to being competitive or uncompetitive. When you've done something that proves beyond a shadow of a doubt that you're competitive, then you get the joy. That one brief moment of joy, it can be less than a minute, can make you forget the past three months of frustration. That's the nature of the game. It's all ups and downs like a roller coaster.

Continuing frustration does something to the mind. It hardens you. I don't think it's a conscious process, but it happens. It has further lessons, too. It teaches you to distinguish what is important from what is unimportant; it teaches you to enjoy whatever you have to enjoy, because if you don't there is nothing but frustration. Your mind learns to block the frustration; otherwise you would not survive in this game.

It is not the same at the beginning of your career as it is later.

The nature of the frustration changes. At the beginning it is more desperate: if things are not going well, then they threaten your very existence in the sport. Later on, it is mitigated. It is displeasure magnified to the nth degree, but you have at least survived to suffer that displeasure. Once you're an established driver, you may be frustrated, but the frustration will refer to a race, a test, a week; it will not extend beyond a season because, once established, every driver thinks that next season must be better than the one he has suffered. At the beginning, a frustration may mean that he'll never have another chance.

I've known both kinds.

Hope is what keeps you going. Better days are coming. The eternal siren song. In the beginning, that's just an assumption. You have no evidence it's going to be so. It's just something you sell yourself. Or try to. In my early days, I didn't often succeed in selling myself hope. In that case, frustration is a killer.

Luckily for me, it's always stayed out of the cockpit. Or nearly always. Even at the beginning, when times were so difficult that I'd climb into the car not knowing if I was going to continue after I got out of it, I was still able to do the driving as driving should be done. Then I'd get out of the cockpit and the world would collapse around me.

In the cockpit I simply ignored the fact that I was fighting a hopeless fight for a result, to qualify, to get the car to work. Once I climbed into the car it was as if I knew that the only thing to do was to take it out and do the best job I could with it. Frustration would lead me to drive harder than I do now; I was trying to wrest that result, that time, from a car that wouldn't give it to me. I always try hard, but today there's a limit. Back then I could go twice over the limit and get that car round by brute force: I suppose that's how frustration creeps into the cockpit. Nothing else worked. Only force. The car was stopping me from doing a job I knew I could do. It was keeping me, personally, from fulfilling my ambitions.

In those days frustration was like a wall. My frustrations today are nothing like that, though they're no less real. But I have matured since then. I've come to accept the fact that the material at your disposal is what sets the limits; you know you have to live within those limits and you accept them, because that is part of fulfilling your contract – your contract with yourself and with your team.

Inside, you're a different person. You're no longer saying, 'I know I could be a first-class driver if only I had the means to be one.' You've established yourself in the game. You know you can do the job because you've done it. At first you feel you haven't even been given a bite at the apple. Even if you are firm in your belief in yourself, and are sure that it is only a rubbish car that is keeping you from success, how can you be *sure* that that is all there is to it? After all, what you've done in F3 or in any other formula no longer counts. You forget all that when you come to F1, so different is the territory you're exploring. The past is gone. You have only the frustrations of the present. Even if people remember what a hot shot you were in what you'd done before, a few frustrated months can wipe that right out. 'OK, so he was good in F2,' they say, 'he's just not good enough for F1.' As F1 is the bigger game, so the frustration is bigger and the consequences of frustration more serious.

To be sure, much of the frustration you can turn away by saying it's not really your fault, it's the machine that's at fault. But, as a professional, you can't afford to perform badly. You still have to do your job, whatever the machine. I'm proud of the fact that I don't have off days; however great the frustration, I still go out and do the best I can.

In Long Beach in 1983 Keke had a day of pure frustration. He made a great start, attacked the field, drove brilliantly, and then was involved in an accident – two in fact – which put paid to his chances of winning a race that he, and most, thought he should have won.

There are times when you relive the old frustrations; they take over and you try to do things by force, just as you used to do in the old days. When I went to Long Beach in 1983, I had just been disqualified by the International Auto Sport Federation (FISA) after coming second in Brazil, a result I'd fought for and burned myself out for. I thought to myself, Keke, you are going to win at Long Beach and show those bastards at FISA. It was the second year running I'd been disqualified in Brazil and I was angry.

Anyway, Keke was going to win Long Beach! Keke was quick!

53

Boy, was he quick! Then I had a spin on the first lap. The ostensible reason for the spin was something beyond my control, a bump on the track; but the real reason was that I was trying to do a leg-breaking act which simply wasn't on. Later, Jarier put me out of the race. Frustration again. There goes Keke's win. But I can be put out of a race any weekend in the year, and I still race the same way. I see now that part of motor racing is learning to accept that there are many things beyond your control. Most things are beyond your control. You can't control the weather, the circuit, the condition of your car, what somebody else does.

What can you control? You can control what you yourself do. One day it is 100 per cent driver; another day it is very little the driver and a lot the car. But even when it's the car, it's still under my control. I still have to fight one way or another to improve my position, as I have to fight to make a poorly functioning car into a better functioning one.

You do this in qualifying, you do it during the race; a lot of the time you do it in testing. That's how you get the equipment to do the job you're paid to do. And if you can't get equipment where you are, then you scheme to move to another team where you can get what you need.

That's a frustration in itself, because it isn't easy in F1 to get the equipment. There aren't that many places to find it; nor can you always tell ahead of time who's going to have it. The sport is full of good drivers who never found it.

I was lucky to get the Williams drive. On the day I was lucky. I got the drive and that happened to be at a time when they had the equipment with which to win the championship; it was still there from the time when Alan Jones won. To some extent drivers construct their own luck. Even in the moments of greatest frustration you must keep working at improving your lot. You have to develop your own skills and somehow work your way into the right position. I'd been in touch with Frank Williams for years before I got the drive with him. Every time he had a seat available, I would call. I'm sure my persistence had something to do with my ultimately getting the drive. I kept working at it; I thought, If I don't get it now, I'll get it one day.

A lot of the time you simply have to train your mind to block out the frustrations, or you would get nothing done. Frustrations on the track are the easiest to block out because at least you're doing something. But, off the track, it's another matter.

Take politics, for instance. I was fined $2000 for crossing a white line at Monza. At the start. The irony of it! At the drivers' briefing the same morning I had told the officials that what they were trying to do was impossible. Like all drivers in F1, I know the narrowing road in Monza. And, like everyone else, I remember the way Ronnie Peterson died. Also, I approve of safety. Name me a driver who doesn't. But to keep all the cars at the start between two white lines is impossible.

If the sporting authority really wants to keep a track confined to a certain predetermined width so that *no* one in *any* circumstances can go outside it, then they should build a wall, because no driver's going to try going through a wall. I told them that. I said, 'What if someone stalls on the grid? How is anyone supposed to get around a driver stalled on the grid? Is he supposed to shoot out into the mainstream of the traffic and cause an accident? What if someone hesitates? What if someone misses a shift? You can't see that sort of thing from outside. So, stuff your regulations. Drivers will do what they have to do. Safety is in their interests. They do the driving. They are grown men, and you shouldn't have rules that you can't enforce.'

So, who crossed the white line at the start? Me. Who got stuffed? Me. I was hopping mad. I had made a good start, then the driver in front of me hesitated. I had to take an instant decision. Which way do I go? I decided to go wide.

Then they come back at me and say, 'Yes, Mr Rosberg, we can understand that, but you stayed on the wrong side of that white line for twenty yards or more.' I certainly did. And why rush back? The most dangerous thing you can do at the start is to join the queue too fast. The idea is to find your spot and fit in. That way there is no danger, no harm is done to anyone. When I watch the film of the race, I see another car with both its wheels on the grass, and there's a white line on that side of the track, too. Does the driver get penalized? No. Only Rosberg got penalized. Once again he'd opened his big mouth. They probably needed the money for a junket to the Ivory Coast or somewhere.

How many times do we see drivers out of the imaginary grid at the start of a race? How many have their wheels on the grass? There are a hundred reasons besides gaining an advantage to take an escape route outside the pack. Which is more dangerous: getting out of trouble – even if it means crossing a white line – or causing an accident by shifting too quickly in and out of a queue? If I cause a dangerous situation because I break a rule, all right, but if I break a rule (which is stupid anyway) to avoid a dangerous situation, is that the same thing?

Have the motor racing authorities got something against me? Yes, they probably have. I'm a cocky bastard. That's what they think and they're probably right. Things like that don't seem to happen to French or Italian drivers. Frustrating? You're damn right. All my experience tells me not to have much faith in the governing body of this sport.

I'm too old to fight against the world, and in F1 the world is FISA. They own the sport, lock, stock and barrel. Why should I make myself sick over one bad decision when I've had so many. Yes, it rankles. There are bureaucrats in Paris who've never faced the start of a race in their lives, and they tell me what to do when it's *my* place, *my* car, *my* life, *my* skills that are on the line. They tell me what to do with those few microseconds in which I have to make a decision. Not just a decision, but the right decision.

I could cause myself two years of bitterness, but why bother? It doesn't mean that the bitterness won't emerge in some other way. As soon as someone turns his back on me, I'll slip the knife in in some other way. I believe in an eye for an eye. I'm not bitter; I am calculating.

The only reason I went to the FISA prize-giving after winning the championship is the $10,000 fine I'd get if I didn't. So I arrive at the ceremony – the prize they're giving was *my* prize, remember! – and the whole business is in French. That really got up my nose. English is the language of motor racing. It's the only language everyone in the sport understands. I decided that if they were going to speak in their own language, why shouldn't I? I was very moderate. Too moderate. I only spoke a few minutes in Finnish. Just to make my point. That's what I wanted to do: just to see what they would do about it, just to watch the expression on their faces. Unfortunately, I couldn't keep a straight face long enough. I started in four languages, went on in Finnish and then wished everyone good night in four languages again, thanking them for their attention.

But that sort of thing is part of the frustration, too. Both my Brazilian disqualifications have been utterly ridiculous.

The first disqualification concerned an issue that was to stay with the sport for several seasons: the use of water as ballast. Rosberg and Piquet were deprived of first and second places in Rio de Janeiro at the beginning of 1982 and their appeal against the decision was denied later in the year. In Keke's case, the decision deprived him of the psychological advantage of an early lead in the championship. The second time, in 1983, Keke again lost six points in Brazil. This time for an infringement of the rule that a car in the pit lane must be started by auxiliary power. When Keke's car came in to refuel and change tyres, there was a brief (but frightening) flash fire as the fuel was being put in under pressure. Keke kept his moustache safe by leaping out of the car, but when he tried to restart, he had to be pushed by the Williams mechanics.

Frustration over the rules – and more particularly with the interpretation of the rules by FISA, the sport's governing body – is widespread in F1. There are few drivers among the British-based teams who feel that FISA interprets the rules fairly; and probably none who think that the procedures used by FISA to sort out interpretative difficulties are appropriate. To anyone used to due legal process in England, the lack of attention to conflicting evidence, the lack of proper notification, the failure to pay attention to expert witnesses and the general 'railroading' of the proceedings smack of arbitrary power.

The first time I got stuffed in Brazil – in 1982 – was over the water tanks. The next year it was back to Brazil again. We studied the regulations with care, in advance. It was the first time we were going to make a pit stop and we discussed all the possibilities in advance. The question was raised, what if I stalled while leaving the pits? We got out the little yellow book and studied the rules. We decided it would probably be quicker to push the car than start playing with the starter cables and everything else again. So when there was a quick flash fire, I jumped out, the fire was put out, the refuelling completed – in all it took about a minute – and because we'd decided everything in advance, no one gave the matter much thought. The mechanics pushed the car because the engine wasn't running. That's the quick way, the efficient way. And aren't men pushing a car an 'outside force' as the regulations say? That's what we'd decided.

The background to this second stuffing is what burns me. We knew we were fast in Brazil. We had been testing there and were eighth fastest officially, but we knew we were faster than that: our own timers had been at the hairpin, not in front of the pits. To fool the rest. So we knew we were quickest. I set pole position. That was an incredible pleasure for me. It was stuff the turbos, stuff everyone saying 'Keke won the championship last year because he was lucky! 1982 was gone, 1983 was a different year. It was going to be a much harder year, and to get pole position in the first race was a hell of an achievement: the last pole position for a Cosworth engine!

I had a hell of a race, too, after the fire. I came back out of the pits after the fire and went right through the field to finish second. It was one of the best races I've ever run. No one cared about that in Paris. No one thinks about it, except me. And I get disqualified on a stupid technicality.

Surely somewhere in Paris or somewhere in the world there has to be someone to ask, 'Did he gain from being pushed or didn't he?' And shouldn't someone consider that the poor bastard they're so busy disqualifying managed to avoid a fire and still went out and did a fantastic race? Wasn't it in their power, yet again, to clarify the rule but not disqualify a hard-earned result?

Later on in the year, Niki reversed in the pit lane at Hockenheim. Disqualification. I agree there. Bloody dangerous to drive backwards on the track or in the pit lane. But if he'd been *pushed* backwards, he wouldn't have been disqualified. That's official, from FISA. What the hell is the sense of that?

Keke accepts that there have to be rules and that someone has to administer them. Some drivers have proposed that a prominent ex-driver should be made commissar – in the American style: someone like Jackie Stewart or Didier Pironi, or Lauda when he finishes racing, would at least understand the technical problems of the sport, be able to relate them to racing and also see things more from a driver's and a sporting point of view.

I have been stuffed by the authorities four times now. I don't want to run the sport and I don't think a driver should run it. Nor do I think it ought to be left to the constructors. A board elected from those who do the actual competing might solve the problem, but it's not uppermost in my mind. I know that little bureaucrats from tiny countries where motor racing doesn't exist shouldn't run it or make decisions about the future of F1 and the people who compete in it.

For 1984 FISA established a new limitation on fuel. This caused grave problems and halfway through the season Ken Tyrrell was disqualified for the rest of the season for having allegedly tampered with his fuel – though the ostensible reason for disqualification was that he had used illegal ballast. The difficulty lay in the fact that enforcing a limitation on fuel was very difficult. When the season began, in Brazil, FISA announced that the local sporting authorities would be in charge of establishing that all teams were within the limits.

That was a typically idiotic FISA decision. If FISA makes a rule, the least they can do is administer it themselves. The teams can't do it: they are interested parties and, anyway, we don't know how to. Williams sent FISA a telex in September 1983 after the new rules were published. The telex said: 'We acknowledge receipt of your rule about fuel consumption. Please can you tell us how controls are going to be established.' Williams never got a reply. And FISA couldn't answer him, because they didn't know themselves.

It's easy for me to criticize, since I don't have a solution; but it is also far too easy for them to make a rule without having any means of ensuring compliance. Constructors know the problem, and they know the bad publicity that will accrue if they can't sort out the problem. I would far rather they eliminate the fuel rule entirely. Better to have a known problem than to enter a grey area in which no one can foresee what the consequences will be. Half the season was dominated, until all the teams solved the problem – each in its own way – by the question of fuel consumption. That merely detracted from the sport.

Furthermore, the rule is poor value for the spectator. It is one more factor which the poor baffled fan has to take into account as he watches his little bit of the race. It's even difficult for us to figure out. Let's say a driver underestimates his fuel consumption: he goes like hell for twenty laps and then suddenly realizes that he's getting into trouble and slows down. What is the spectator going to make of that? Or another driver realizes he's being too conservative, and suddenly he's off like the blazes. The fan will never know what really happened. That's not good for the sport.

Someone has to make the rules. But you can't make a rule in Paris and expect it to be controlled in another country by someone else. Not in any fair way.

Being the kind of man I am, I would prefer to have no rules at all, or the very minimum of rules. Just the overall measurements of the car and tell everyone to go for it. What I object to in the sport's administration is that FISA can favour some and disfavour others, because if it can do that, history tells me it will disfavour me.

Anyway, I find politics a total waste of time. I'm so busy driving cars in circles I haven't got the time to worry about who gets elected in FISA. I'm sure FISA are under all sorts of pressures, national and otherwise. So far as I know, I've never been disqualified *because* I am a Finn. I've been disqualified because of my ugly face or my big mouth. The result is the same.

The truth is that I don't give a damn about politics: as long as they don't involve me directly. I couldn't care less. I know that my way of handling this problem is entirely wrong. I sit here criticizing someone but I would hate to have to do something about it. I don't have any public conscience. I don't have the right motives. Lauda sometimes makes an effort to better a track or improve driver safety. But I'm not completely sure of his motives either. When he came into F1 he was the most active of spokesmen; now perhaps he has less time to worry about such matters.

I don't belong to any organization or group, I don't wear a uniform, I don't take sides. I am not a political man; the welfare of mankind is not my business. That shocks some people. They would like to put a stamp on my head saying, 'Keke says this, but really he's a moral man.' I don't know what a moral man is. I live as I believe is right. As I've learned to live at home, as I've been raised, as I've raised myself, as I've learned in my lonely past to live. Those are the only rules I live with.

When I got disqualified at Monza, I was prepared to spend a few thousand dollars of my own money to finance a world-wide story on FISA. I thought a larger number of people should know what they were up to, and believe me, it would have made interesting reading. It would have been sweet revenge in a way; he was on water skis and couldn't have cared less. The frustration passed.

Guilt

The progress of conversations about a driver's life is not always stately or smooth. There are places where themes cross and understanding is difficult to reach. At such points it is valuable to set the record down in its own dramatic context.

The subject is guilt. The scene: Ibiza, dockside, Keke's boat, a trip into the blue Mediterranean. I introduce the subject of selfishness. The man has a large portion of the world's goods for himself. What is uppermost in his mind is the enjoyment of his toys. He feels he needs them. What is he not thinking about when he is enjoying those toys?

Q. Back to selfishness. Priorities are important. They are part of professional life.

A. Everything has to be calculated and planned. I don't leave anything to chance if I can help it. Yes, priorities are very important.

Q. Thus when you talk about risks, you mean you take those risks which are necessary to achieve a particular aim.

A. I do things the professional way. It is demanded of me and of all drivers to be highly selfish. That selfishness that I have to use professionally spills over into other areas as well. You live in your private environment and that becomes more than a little selfish. It *is* a question of priorities. Only when you've got past the first priority can you pay attention to the second. The first priority may be racing or business; the second may be a human priority. You may not get around to that human priority; you may neglect it. That is a more honest explanation than saying that you don't get around to your human priorities because you're too selfish to bother. It may be that you don't have any energy left after you've taken care of number one.

Q. At least you don't suffer any guilt. That is already something.

A. If I start feeling guilty because I haven't done something, I block my brain off. I get it out of my system as quickly as possible and before it bothers me. I can't have guilt getting in the way of total commitment.

Q. Thus you have no guilt in life at all?

A. No, I expect everybody else, everyone around me, to understand how my priorities are established. That includes my parents, sister, anyone around me. I expect them to understand total commitment as I understand it.

Q. And therefore not to make demands on you that you could not meet?

A. And make me feel guilty. Right. Exactly right. My parents have always coped with this situation extremely well. I can't even get them excited about anything any more. They accept that what I do is what I do. When I called my father and said I'd signed for another two years with Williams, I was thinking, Isn't that terrific! And what did he say? He said, 'Well, I thought you would.' Here we are talking about what is, in Finnish terms, a hell of a lot of money. There are probably very few people in Finland earning what I earn. I expected him to get excited. Nothing. I said, 'This means I'll be making so much over the next two years.' He said, 'Ah, that's all right then.'

Q. Supposing he had said the contrary? Supposing he'd said that wasn't enough, he might feel he was making a demand on you. He's smart enough to leave well enough alone.

A. He would never say that. I lead my own life, my parents lead their own lives. We're very close. I know they still love my sport and enjoy every success I have.

Q. Your father's proud of you.

A. Yes, he is. I've done something he would have loved to do.

Q. Perhaps you feel guilty about that? What I suspect is that he's pleased you've stayed yourself.

A. From his point of view, I may not have. As a Finn, he probably thinks I'm a little crazy. But you have to remember, by now by far the most important part of his life is my racing and his own family; he lives very intensely everything that I do.

Q. That means you share it with him. Then you're not as selfish as you say. I wonder if he thinks you've changed?

A. I'm sure he'd say I have. I have changed a lot since leaving home. It's obvious. One matures, one changes. It's just that F1 matures you pretty fast.

Q. A lot of money often goes to people's heads. You haven't changed that much. A boat, a plane, but no conspicuous consumption, no fancy women, no playboying around.

A. If that's what defines money going to somebody's head, that's right. That's never been my bag. You'll never see me flashing money around, losing £3000 on a single throw of the dice at backgammon. I don't need to impress people by throwing money around or by having a wild party. I don't like to throw money away because it's been a hard job earning it. My accountant worries: why don't I ever spend money? No, the heart of our business, or any business, is that money is important. You are always trying to make more of it. That would be exactly the same if I were running a conventional business. I would always be trying to double what I have. I would be trying to use all the possibilities that the business offered.

But there's always one thing in the back of my mind. That everything I do be 100 per cent correct and legal. I don't want anyone coming in later years and saying, 'Hey, how about that year? Did you pay your taxes?' I can always plan tomorrow because I know that yesterday is not going to offer me a nasty surprise.

Q. That's called having a conscience.

A. I don't care what it's called. I'm such an honest bastard, I don't need to have a guilty conscience about such matters, or about anything.

Q. Still, you have a conscience.

A. I wouldn't know. I've never put it to the test.

Q. Would you behave deliberately badly towards someone who cared for you?

A. Definitely not. Why should I hurt somebody? When you talk about conscience, you're talking about yourself suffering as a consequence of something you've done.

Q. That's not what conscience is.

A. Now you're trying to teach me English.

Q. Conscience is what keeps you from doing evil. It must happen often enough in races: when you know that something you might do could be dangerous to another driver so you don't do it. Or is it solely because if you hurt another driver you stand a good chance of being hurt yourself? Conscience or enlightened self-interest?

A. If I have a braking competition with another driver at a corner, if I out-brake him and go through the corner with the wildest slide of my life and he goes off without us touching, then I'd have one of the best laughs of my life. As long as he isn't hurt.

Q. Conscience has a role in sport. You all know each other. If you hurt someone, you'd feel guilty. If you'd done it deliberately.

A. It makes me tired to talk about subjects I don't understand.

6

The World Opens Up

Christmas, 1976. Fred Opert on the telephone. 'My driver has dropped out: can you race in New Zealand?' That was the beginning of two years of frantic racing on all the continents of the world. First was the successor to the old Tasman series, rebaptized Peter Stuyvesant. The cars were Formula Pacific: all Ford BDA 1.6-litre engines and 215 b.h.p. Keke was right at it on 3 January. He started with a retirement at Bay Park, but the following week led from start to finish of the New Zealand Grand Prix at Pukehoke near Auckland. His car was a Cotter-Ford Chevron. He registered another start-to-finish victory at Manfield. The fourth race, at Teretonga, gave the same result. In the last race, he finished a mere second, which was enough to win the Tasman series. It was quite a beginning to 1977.

Meanwhile, Keke had renewed his contract with Obermoser's F2 Toj team. A new car, the Toj F201 was ready in February; it was an immediate disappointment. Never one to let grass grow under his feet, Keke talked to Fred Opert who had said after New Zealand that although previously he had always considered Villeneuve the best driver in Formula Atlantic, he had now changed his mind. No one was as good as Keke Rosberg. But money was again a problem: a contract was ready if Keke could raise some money. Time was short. Thanks to the arrival in the team of an American Super Vee driver, Wink Bancroft, as Keke's number two, the contract was signed. Keke's opportunities multiplied: Opert had signed him for no fewer than twenty-six races in eleven months: fifteen in F2, five in Canada in Formula Atlantic, the Macao Grand Prix, and a repeat performance in New Zealand at the beginning of 1978.

It took him three races to notch up his first point, at Thruxton.

Not good enough. I was shoved off the track by an Italian and I didn't have time to catch up again. Only victory counts and that's what I had to aim for. With results like these I had no hope of getting into F1 the following year, and that's what I wanted.

The next race at the Nürburgring, Keke was third. The results were an interesting presage: Mass, Cheever, Rosberg, Pironi, Arnoux, Giacomelli. Vallelunga: eighth. Then a race across the Atlantic. Mosport: Keke v. Villeneuve. After a tangle described elsewhere, Keke's engine blew.

My world had collapsed. In getting into F1 Villeneuve was the man to beat. A victory over Gilles would have been manna from heaven.

Bad luck continued at Pau in F2: at Pau his shock absorbers went after several brushes with his rivals. Back to Canada, to Giml: second place. Then Mugello: his engine gave up the ghost. He complained of ill fortune. Canada again, and Edmonton: a spectacular struggle with Villeneuve, and Keke finished second. Back in Europe, Nogaro – no result. Westwood: victory at last. Keke led the championship, 78 points to 54 for Villeneuve, who was behind Rahal and Brack. Had luck changed? At the Lago di Pergusa a victory at last in F2. Then Canada again: Halifax, he retired; Saint Felicien, a near-fatal crash; Trois Rivières, and three of the first five places in practice went to Opert cars: Rosberg, Depailler and Laffite. But Keke shunted with Villeneuve and retired. Finally, Quebec. Keke was third in the championship table behind Brack and Villeneuve. Keke led with Villeneuve on his tail; Keke spun and dropped back to third; on lap 10, Bobby Rahal shoved Keke off the circuit. Villeneuve champion.

F2 finished in Europe. Pironi won in Estoril, but behind him Arnoux, Cheever and Keke fought it out, finishing within a second of each other. Arnoux's second place made him European F2 champion; Keke was sixth. Six more points at Donington fail to change that position. As an afterthought, Suzuka in Japan in a Renault F2: retirement after two laps. Holidays in Thailand and the Grand Prix of Macao: another retirement. Willie Kauhsen, who had brought Keke to Japan, negotiated with Kojima for an F1 car for Keke: it would have been his first F1 race. It wasn't to be.

The balance for this season of phenomenal activity – it was to be exceeded by 1978 – was twenty-six races, five pole positions, five vic-

tories, six other placings: sixth in F2, fourth in Formula Atlantic and first in Formula Pacific. 1978 looked promising.

Human Relations

It is well-known of the sport that, within it, human relations are rarer than radium: harder to make, harder to weave, harder to keep. The strains of the sport are extreme; so is its egocentricity. It is all very well that the F1 family travels together, eats together, hotels together, drives together, works together; the truth is that in this case the family that plays together does not stay together.

Drivers live in compartmented worlds. If one observed Lauda and Prost in 1984, one heard protestations of friendship; one was aware of rivalry and tension. The two men shared a motor-home and a team; they had with each other an easy camaraderie, such as all people in dangerous occupations – like men in trenches – share with each other. But friendship is a different quality. The people in F1 live within carefully circumscribed areas: engineers do their thing, team managers manage, drivers drive, mechanics stay up all night and do what they're asked, sponsors sponsor. There is little overlap between these different areas and no solitude as great as that of the driver alone in his machine. There, he is beyond the reach of anyone. He is in a private world of his own. As Lauda once said on getting out of a car and required to perform a simple straightforward task, his head was still going at 200 k.p.h. It is not any easier to adjust down than it is to adjust up.

Thus friendships are often outside things. Most drivers have friends, intimate friends, who are outside the sport. It is somewhat easier that way. It may be easier, too, to have a wife who is outside the sport. Which does not mean for a second that drivers do not need or value friendship as much as other sportsmen or human beings in general. It is just that those friendships are bound to be frailer than the ordinary run of friendships. Time, distance, risk and the high specialization of the profession make that evident. The further a driver progresses in the sport, the less likely it is that a friend can share – with either intimacy or understanding – the heartland. That heartland is impenetrable. It is made of ego, of fear, of ambition, of desire, of a whole series of elements that are alien to the average man.

Human relations count for more than anything; at the same time, nothing is more difficult to maintain. All the success and wealth in the world would be pointless without friends. But true friendship in this sport is hard to come by. One is too busy polishing the apple with *important* friends, with those who can do something for you, to keep up with friends you personally care for far more.

I have to trust that my friendships are well enough and deeply enough laid so that they will survive this difficult period in which I have to neglect them.

In a way, it is a test of true friendship: the true friends will remain and the less true ones will drift away, feeling neglected. I don't think the sacrifice that is asked of them is fair. It isn't fair on me, either. I would prefer to have my friends about me. But how can I explain to every single person I care about why I haven't found the time to see them in two years? They're home every night at six on the dot. How can they understand my life? How can I say, listen, I just don't have the time to come and see you? Even if I do take the time to explain, they can't really believe me.

Nobody can imagine what life is like on the inside who isn't on the inside. They read in their papers that I'm just back from Ibiza. Well, they ask, why hasn't he at least called? Why did he go to Ibiza instead of coming through Helsinki or London and having a friendly dinner with me, the way he used to do in the old days? They don't know that if I go to Ibiza it's because I am too smashed, too tired, too exhausted to do anything else. They don't understand that, literally, I don't want to do anything. I don't want to think, I don't want to see anyone. I just want to recover my forces. Not just my physical strength, but also my mind.

My privacy has become ever more valuable and important to me. As you go on, you're less and less able to cope with the world of driving unless you have that privacy to go back to. It's the great big repair shop of the mind and the body. I have a plane because it allows me access to more of that privacy; I have even less that I share with other people.

That may be true of life in general, but it is especially true of my profession: a driver is in the middle of it all, all the time. He is nagged from left and right; he cannot breathe. If there were nothing else, there are the crowds, the sheer mass of people. I hardly ever work on my own. Only in a race.

I shall never forget once going to Monza to test. When I left the pits and drove onto the track there wasn't anyone there but me. It was beautiful. I was the happiest man in the world. I don't think anyone else can imagine that feeling.

But how far down the road is a man when he thinks like that? When his pleasure is to be driving fast alone in a park in Monza? If that's where he finds peace? And the only pressure on him is to improve his car and drive fast? What sort of man is reduced to that? Where are the rest of the world's pleasures?

There are other ways of finding privacy and peace, of course. But you have to find them first; and then you have to enjoy those occasions, to struggle against weariness and mental exhaustion. I spend all my time working and thinking; I have no energy left for talk or for society.

I may have exhausted my mental reserves. I don't know. The best is to light a fire, sit down on the floor and stare at the flames. That's how far down the road I am. That's why privacy starts counting for more and more. The opposite of privacy is representation. To be someone for someone else. I represent myself, my sponsors, my team: always I represent instead of existing.

It isn't so much resentment as a mental block that builds up. I enjoy setting down my life and thoughts, but when I finish, it is with relief. In the same way, friends are a joy, but they deprive me of my privacy, and I am split; perhaps I no longer really know what I want.

Work, Work

First the racing, the driving. That's the part you can't and don't want to avoid. That's the love. That's the bread. That's the job.

Then there's your own commercial development. You can pass that up if you want to. Piquet and I have a good understanding. I understand the way he operates. When he's through with the things he *has* to do, he messes about on a boat or rests or fixes things. He understands the way I work. I couldn't do it his way; he couldn't do it mine. It's not that I wouldn't like to sit around on a boat doing nothing between engagements. I'd love it. But I go about things my own way.

If I ran a shoe store and I needed to sell five and a half pairs a day to break even, I'd be an idiot to close my doors every day when I'd sold five and a half pairs of shoes. Next day the weather might be lousy and no one would come to my store. So I have to sell as much as possible each day.

If I lived the way Nelson does, I'd be thinking all the time that opportunity was passing me by. I don't only mean the chance to make more money, I mean the chance to learn more. I learn a lot from marketing people. That's an opportunity which might come good for me one day.

Everyone thinks it's money, money, money. It isn't. No man in his right mind would work as hard as I do just for money.

Perhaps I'll say to myself, 'Listen, one day you're going to stop driving in F1.' It might be because I'm fed up with travelling, or I don't have the stamina any more. Then, I'd argue with myself. 'Look, do what you like doing now the most, which is driving. Get yourself a good contract, show up at the first race with a clean pair of overalls and drive. You can think about later later.' Well, I know me. The first day I'd start thinking, Hell, you've got some time to spare. Why don't you do something? I'd be right back in the same situation. For me there is no other way of doing it than the way I do it right now. Either I do it this way or I don't do it at all.

The racing life is a short life. If the average career at the top is something like ten to twelve years (and that's for the survivors and for those who do make it to the top, or near), then five of those will have gone before you even get a chance to drive in F1. Another two or three will go before you get in among the select few who are invited to drive for the teams where the real money – and therefore the real success – is. That leaves you four or five years at the top: against which you have to reckon the very real chance that you might not make it to the very top (there's only one champion per year and seven champions in the past ten years – Lauda, Andretti, Scheckter, Piquet, Hunt, Jones and Rosberg – and four of those have retired from F1) or that, having arrived there, you might be the victim of an accident like Villeneuve or Pironi, like Peterson or Depailler or Jabouille. In F1 you make your pile while the sun shines. And for that you can pay a high price. You might not be living at all.

It isn't that all the outside activities take up a big part of your mind. Frankly, they don't take up very much space in my brain. But for me racing is one big picture, and the commercial work is part of that picture. Commercial work, promotional work. Your average fan probably thinks there's nothing to promotion. What he doesn't reckon is the time it takes. Even if all you're doing is lending your name to something, it takes time. There's time negotiating, discussing. My manager does that, but I still have to go through it with him. Then at the very least there are the pictures to be taken: holding a racquet, a can of beer, whatever. That photo session has to be fitted in somewhere. I have to be available. The studio has to be free. I have to get there.

All right, that looks easy enough. But then it's complicated by the fact that the team and my driving have the absolute priority. My manager can set up the best schedule in the world, but if Frank Williams calls up and says, 'Keke, I'll need you at Paul Ricard next Tuesday,' forget it. I take very good care of the people I make promotional deals with, but they too understand that Williams comes first. That's the basis of my independence within Williams. That's part of the package you negotiate before you sign on. One of the reasons why I signed with Williams is that they gave me the freedom to do other things. It's important to me to function: not just in the car, but in all those other ways.

The Times, They Are A'changing

Drivers know about the past, the past that journalists keep alive, only from legend and anecdote. With a few exceptions, they are a remarkably un-historical bunch. There is no tradition in motor racing, just a few survivors from earlier days, people with long memories. If you drive for Ferrari, you get caught up in that legend: because the old man, Enzo, is still around and he's a direct link with that past. The same was true for Colin Chapman when he was still alive – though, unlike Enzo Ferrari, Chapman was never a sentimentalist about the past. Bernard Ecclestone, who owns Brabham, remembers some drivers he liked particularly (they drove for him) but is sentimental about nothing. And Ken Tyrrell, for whom everyone seems to have driven at one time or another, is still around.

A more significant point to make, however, is that there are times in a driver's career when that sort of sentiment is tedious. Today's driver is a now man. Or a tomorrow man. If someone looks too much into the past, it's an obstacle to development, to the future. Old ideas exist to be discarded and F1 is a perfectly disposable world. FISA could change the rules tomorrow and say F1 consisted of perambulators from Harrods being wheeled about the Serpentine and that would be that: finis *to the past. Keke found that out working with some of his constructors; he, too, is a man relatively without sentiment.*

I don't know what relations used to be like among drivers. I wasn't around. In the time I've been around they haven't changed one iota. Not the human relationships.

But remember, I came in at the end of an era. Back then there were a lot of people living next to each other and off enthusiasm. Back then, so they tell me, there were only ten races a year. You didn't do any testing. You had all the time in the world to socialize. There were no personal sponsors; or, if you had one, the most he might ask of you was to lead off the ball once a year.

To start with, we don't live close to each other any more. You get one driver living in Switzerland, another in Austria, a third in Spain, another in England and so on. Monte Carlo is about the only place where there is more than one driver.

Even on the circuits, drivers are a lot busier than they used to be and there's no great reason for us to see each other at dinners. Within a team, yes. But usually that's obligation. It's all the Renault dealers from Detroit or something like that: in which case you put on your jacket and tie and get on with the other side of your work. You see your fellow-drivers in the paddock, but that's in passing. You live very much with your team-mate at the track, but the relation between team-mates is a different sort of friendship. You see your friends – by which I mean those drivers you like more than others – more at some places than others: for instance, at the more remote circuits, where there's always more time, in South Africa, Brazil.

But outside the circuit itself, top drivers don't have that much time. My life is part Williams, part myself. I race for Williams, I test for Williams, I may do a lot of other small things for Williams, but the rest of the time I have a lot of other things to do for companies that might be related to racing but also might not be. That takes time.

Hence the accusation that drivers are no longer the 'characters' they once were: though, even there, there is a suspicion that just how egregious those 'characters' of former days were is now covered with a rose-coloured haze. There are splendid stories, but most of them have to do with on-track activities, particular private defiances of the laws of averages, snooks cocked at authorities (which were a lot less authoritarian then than they are now), quarrels with team owners, rivalries between individual drivers. As many as appear to have been larger than life, there was still a majority who, in retrospect, look no more than life size, or less than life size. The rest is invention, nostalgia. It may have seemed a freer time than it actually was. And the heart of that appearance was probably that drivers felt themselves to be freer than they are now. Certainly, they had fewer outside preoccupations. Today's driver's attaché case is the perfect metaphor: money means accounting, logistics, travel, arrangements, deals.

I know people say there are no characters left. Rubbish. You're a character in a different way. Alan Jones was a character. Gilles Villeneuve was a character. Niki Lauda's a character. They're just different sorts of character.

If I had only the races to do each year – as it was in the old days – which is the *visible* part of what a driver does, then the public would see the emergence of the kinds of 'characters' they seem to long for. People would see my private life as well as my public. I'd go skiing, I'd play sports, I might even enjoy myself a bit. That's what a 'character' is, someone people see all the time and everywhere. The ones the gossip columns follow.

My wife might have time to run away with someone else, because she'd be sitting at home a lot more; and maybe at home she'd get bored. Not the way we live our life. We're on the same planes, in the same hotels.

The world has changed. I won't be drawn into saying for better or worse. I will say, we work a hell of a lot harder.

Body

The mind is pushed to the limits. The body is pushed even further. Drivers look fit; they are fit. Most are fitness freaks – from Lauda's special diets to Laffite's endless sport, to the lonely runners. A very special stamina is required. It is the driver's body which must produce it. It is his body which is used. In its hostile environment used and punished. Locked up in a tiny vibrating cockpit. Driven by an engine of awesome power. Riding on a a suspension that feels every scratch in the surface.

Driving a race car is like fighting a war against yourself. It is as though you were waging war on your body, and the body takes a hell of a beating. You are in this sport for the fun of it, because you like it, love it, want it; you remember that when the temperature is up around 100 degrees in Rio, and you wonder. Driving a car in those conditions – and no conditions are ever perfect; in almost every situation there is some special difficulty – is somewhere way beyond fun. To survive, you have to have a special determination. It is war. A war in which the elements are against you and your body is weak.

Everything is against you. Every man on the track is after you. The heat is after you. You live in a world of total hostility.

Are we all masochists? I wonder. I jog. I do it because I get paid to keep fit to do my job properly, but that's for masochists too. Once it's over, you get your little ration of pleasure. You've done something which is no fun, and we're taught that not all the valuable things in life are fun.

On the other hand, there are compensations when things go well, or when you think they're going to go well. Then all the cars ahead of you aren't so hostile; each of them is something you're going to overtake. You no longer struggle, you're achieving something for yourself. That gives you pleasure, though you don't have time to think about it. You get past one, you mark down a mental cross, then another and another. Those are the good moments.

But the body still suffers. It suffers all the time. I cannot imagine any other situation in which I would push myself as hard as I do in a race.

There are so many things that can hurt. Heat is one of them, though it probably bothers me less than most people. In Monaco in 1903 it was my hands. I went through the first layer of skin and onto the second. It hurt. And at the end I had no skin at all. There I was in gloves, but the pull of the wheel is such the hands move inside the gloves. Maybe I have ladylike hands. The car kicks every time you go over a bump. Most of the time you have to grip the wheel as hard as you can. Some circuits are smooth and dainty, like Paul Ricard; even when they're smooth, you still grip hard. It's worse on the hands since the big wings came back. The cars are heavy with fuel and the wings make them that much heavier to move around; it takes real strength sometimes just to hold the wheel.

In 1982 we used to start the races on very low tyre pressures – especially with Goodyears, which had a tendency to build up a lot of pressure and lose their shape because they weren't then radials – and in two or three races I went off at the first corner after the start because the cars simply were not reacting normally. Someone in the team suggested that I wasn't strong enough to turn the wheel. It is laughable, but that gives an idea of the pressure you use to hold on to the wheel.

A lot of what you suffer physically has to do with your driving technique; and sometimes with the situation in a race, in which there are easy times as well as hard times. But my style of driving is probably more wearing than Niki's. Playing defensive tennis is less taxing than playing attacking tennis.

With muscles you can't tell where the problem is: hands, forearms, shoulders, back, neck: they can all hurt. In Rio de Janeiro it's the neck. It's got all those left-hand corners and the neck is better developed on the right. When your neck hurts, that's very specific. Or your clutch foot.

If you think about it, the cockpit is a place you live in for two hours endlessly doing the same motions. It's not the most comfortable home. In the sixties, drivers used practically to lie down. Then the small wings came in and Graham Hill said, 'From now on we're going to have to start practising physically to cope with the tremendous new G-force.' Little did he know.

Everything you do in a car is physical. You shift gears between 1500 and 2500 times, depending on the track and the box you're using. That's a physical effort, however gentle the gears are. If you had to pick up a pencil from a desk 2500 times for an hour, you'd find that a physical effort.

All sorts of things wear you down. Like the noise. The noise is constant and tremendous. Like a woman's knitting club. Worse. Push your earplugs all the way in and it's still noisy. The noise is tiring because it's constant and unvarying. It's like something playing inside you. Listening to anything for that long is tiring.

The eyes get tired. They get tired when the mind gets tired. The eyes are full of all sorts of little tricks the average person wouldn't think about. Your eyes can start watering because your visor is kept a bit open to keep fog from forming. Especially during a wet race. When that happens, there's nothing you can do about it. They can itch. There's nothing you can do about that. Sweat can get into your eyes, which is why I try to keep the balaclava as deep as possible to soak up the sweat. If you open your visor a little when it's wet, you get a stream running out of your eyes. It's better to cry than have a misty visor. However, the wind hits your eyes from top to bottom; it pins your eyelids down.

You complain about the air you're getting in. Although it's cool. It's a lot cooler than the air you get inside your helmet. But then you're stuck with a problem. You want more air? You open your visor a crack. Then if you go into the catch fencing you're going to have catch fencing all over your face. Or keep it closed and sweat more. Monte Carlo, no catch fencing. Zandvoort or Kyalami, catch fencing like a jungle. The choice is yours, the risks are yours. Every part of your body is a potential problem and you have to think about each and every part: before you start, while you're racing and afterwards, when you sometimes feel you'd like to replace the whole lot.

Like legs. Or feet.

I have a foot problem which isn't entirely cured. So does Jacques. It's as though someone had lit a fire under my foot and I can trace the pain all the way up to my head. All I know is it's a terrible pain, and we don't seem to be able to cure it completely, although I've found a guy in Austria who can at least control it.

But you get used to it. You get used to the fact that when you get into a car and race, something is going to hurt.

And then there is remission. Days when everything is right and there's no pain at all. It's a cool day, there are long, easy curves; there are long straights; you have no problems in the world; the race is going well; you've still got the skin on your hands.

But those times are the minority. Sometimes it's the heat. Then you hear your heart going pump, pump, pump. Maybe it's your breathing. That's very difficult for an attacking driver like me, when you're attacking for a long period of time, over a long sequence of corners. Or after practice, when you breathe twice as heavily because you haven't been breathing at all while putting in your qualifying lap.

You don't breathe in a fast corner. Not when it's critical. You don't decide not to breathe; it just happens that you don't. It's at though you're trying to thread a needle; you don't breathe then either; you need all your concentration to get the thread into the eye. I'm sure you don't breathe much during a qualifying lap: you need every bit of your concentration. It's you and the machine out there trying to hammer out just one quick time. Why do we accept a challenge like that?

Those fast laps are very special. They put a special stress on the body as well as the mind. You're travelling faster than you ever will in a race and the effort – of concentration, of every part of the body stressed to achieve just that one thing – is tremendous. It's an incredible effort. After which you return to normal life like a man reprieved.

But would I do without it? No. Why should I be deprived of that pleasure? Why did I become a racing driver? Because I enjoy going around a corner as fast as I humanly can and exposing myself, mind and body, to all the stresses that implies. No one has the right to speak on my behalf. No one can say I'm taking too many risks when I'm qualifying. I'm not. I'm just pushing myself to my limits.

Villeneuve

Driving styles vary, but they're largely determined by mental attitude. The image the world has of my style is that if the door isn't open I'll drive right through it. I'm not sure that it's an exact image, but I'm stuck with it and it suits me. My style of driving really hasn't changed since my earliest days; it is founded upon my desire and determination to go faster. What has changed is my tools. And sometimes, too, conditions on a given day affect my style. There might be a day when I'm very angry; the reasons don't matter, the fact does. I'll drive more angrily. Or on another day I might feel not anger but pleasure. In Rio Nelson and I have had fights that were pure pleasure; in which we passed and repassed each other. We were both doing something well and each felt he knew what the other was doing. Even as we raced against each other, we felt mutual respect.

There are other styles of racing. I can remember René Arnoux and Gilles having a ding-dong, each of them knocking his head against a wall. Both of them had the identical attitude: both of them were going to bang through the door. They were in different teams, but the same thing happened with Gilles and his own team-mates. You can't take that attitude with a team-mate. It takes a brave man to do that with someone from another team; it is foolhardy to do it with someone on the same team, as Gilles did with Didier Pironi in Imola, for instance.

But the fact that Gilles got away with it reflects a difference between Ferrari and other teams. At Ferrari they love that sort of thing. I read an interview with Harvey Postlethwaite, who designs at Ferrari, in which he said that Villeneuve was a fantastic driver: if he had to opt for finishing second in safety or for taking over first place and crashing, Gilles would opt for first place and crash. At Ferrari they think that's a great attitude for a driver to have.

I don't agree. Without wishing to put Gilles down – for he was a great driver – I would say that on any other team he would have got a right bollocking. At Ferrari he was built up as a great hero: even though he crashed or spun when he was leading a race. That's not how champions are made. Still Gilles was a hero of his era.

There are people who criticized Nelson Piquet for letting Patrese past in South Africa when Nelson was trying to make sure he won the world championship, people who say that by not trying to win the race, Nelson let the public down. But the public isn't that stupid. The fact is, Nelson had just one job to do: he had to win the championship – for himself, for Brabham and for BMW. That was his job and he did it outstandingly. People who disagree claim that in the past drivers went out to win every race. That's not what the championship is about. It's great to win races, but our real competition is the world championship. I've spent ten years driving not to win, say, three Brazilian Grands Prix but to win the championship and then have another crack at it. That's why, at the beginning of a season, a driver will go out in search of maximum points; but, towards the end, he will go for the number of points he can safely score to win the championship. That's what Nelson did with Prost in South Africa in 1983, that's what Lauda did, again with Prost, in 1984, and that's what I did in Las Vegas in 1982.

The regulations say the first six get points. To win the championship, you build points. If only first place gave points, we'd all have very powerful engines! That's why I say about Gilles that, fantastic driver though he was, he was not necessarily a champion in the making. First or nothing is not the attitude of a champion.

I raced a lot against Gilles in the beginning. Then we split up. He went to Ferrari in F1 and I was struggling in small teams. But I knew that whatever he could do I could also do. We had endless battles in all sorts of formulas.

The man had guts, skill and intelligence, and I often wonder what would have happened to him if he'd raced for someone other than Ferrari. Either he would have been sacked for writing off too many cars or an English team would have taught him some discipline. An English team would have recognized his indisputably great qualities as a driver but would have given him the kind of discipline he needed to be a champion.

Discipline wouldn't have made him any slower. Gilles's was a natural skill. Unfortunately, the Italians worshipped him. Even if he put a car in the wall, they thought that was terrific.

He took all his races personally. We were in Formula Atlantic together and he was no different. It was as though he had his own personal barrier he wanted to break through. He would shunt one car and five minutes later he'd be out in his spare shunting that. There are other people like Gilles in the sport. My old team-mate Derek Daly is one. They have no fear. Derek may have lacked Gilles's skill but he had the same mental attitude. When Derek flew twenty feet over a billboard in Zandvoort he saw the pictures and thought it was good stuff. It was exciting, he said, and he laughed about it. What he didn't think about was that the car could have landed upside down and that would have been the end of the laughing.

I'm not saying Gilles was like that inside his head. How do you ever know? But he behaved and drove as though that was what he felt.

Take nothing away from him, a great driver. But if you go on like that – if Andrea de Cesaris had continued as he started out – you're asking for trouble. That's why I'm amazed when people think *I* drive like that. I think I'm as self-protective as you can get. Maybe my limit is a bit higher than some people's. Gilles's was probably too high.

I'm not fearless at all. Gilles was.

In the good old days when there was no Armco and Gilles and I were driving the proper flat-out stuff, we were both pretty stubborn. When we met there were usually sparks. But Gilles was so much quicker in his March Atlantic than I was in my Chevron that our fights were a little one-sided.

Sometimes they were hilarious. In Edmonton once, Gilles was leading and I was hauling him in. I knew that with a 'bastard' like Gilles I wasn't going to get too many chances. Then suddenly he made a mistake and I was able to get right up to him and try to pass. I went on the inside of him and we did the whole of a long corner side by side banging into each other. The pair of us ended up off the track on opposite sides and the pair of us still in full swing came back in off the grass and down the bank at full speed at exactly the same spot and banged into each other again. Gilles won, I came second. At the end of the race my car looked like a piece of cake with a big slice taken out of it. My car wasn't damaged but his rear rim had cut through my bodywork all the way into the tub.

Another time, in Mosport in 1977, Gilles was the loser. We came over the brow there banging wheels and we were both in midair, banging wheels, still trying to find out who was going to get to the corner first. Luckily for me, Gilles spun and I went through. I had a good lead in the race and then my engine blew: that was what was always happening to me in those days. As in my 1979 season in Can-Am when I totally dominated the season and only won two or three races despite being on pole position in eight out of nine races!

We don't have many battles like that in F1 these days. We don't race quite so personally. F1 matures you fast.

Gilles was a hard man, but he was also very fair. If you came up alongside him, he would be the last one to brake. I had another great battle with him in Long Beach in 1982. He was in the Ferrari and I was in the Williams. We passed each other four or five times until I finally got him. It was a fair and square battle. We both kept our lines, each tried to brake later than the other, but Gilles out-braked me on the outside, which no one can do on that corner. In the end he only out-braked himself. That was his way of doing things.

I liked him a lot as a driver. I liked the way he raced. No one is perfect and I might, in earlier days, have done what he did at Zandvoort with his rear wheel falling apart while he still kept on driving. Back then I might have taken the same risk. But, by my book, not in F1. His courage was far beyond normal standards.

His death didn't hit me right away. I was in the thick of the championship and although I had a good lead in the Belgian Grand Prix that weekend, I had constantly to put Gilles out of my mind. Then, after the race, physical exhaustion took over, mental exhaustion, disappointment; I was wiped out. It didn't hit me hard until the next morning.

For some reason I drove by the track. I don't know why. I must have been just coming from the hotel. Have you ever been on a track on a Monday morning all on your own? It's the emptiest place in the world. After all that activity and intensity, there's not a soul about. It's dead. Nothing but litter. And parked out there was Gilles's helicopter. Then it hit me. Very hard.

For some reason I still think of German television. They won't show a race live because of the possibility of accidents, to spare their viewers. But for the next few days they showed replays of Gilles's death. Over and over again.

Jones

Alan Jones was a bit like Villeneuve, but he was an even harder 'bastard'. The incident I always remember with Alan was in Can-Am in 1979. I had pole position and a good lead in the race. It came to the last laps and I was trying to lap Geoff Lees. I had no brakes left and Lees wouldn't let me by. I could see Alan catching up and when we reached the big hairpin with grass on the inside, I dug my nose under Lees's wing. What did Alan do? He drove straight into my side and sent me off. The bastard won the race. He was on the inside, so he just leaned on me. It was plain boxing: nothing to do with motor racing. I thought I'd protected myself, because I knew that if I gave him an inch he'd take me on the inside; but I never thought anyone would put four wheels on the grass on the inside and put me off. But he did, and it's his result that stands.

Accidents

Risk is endemic; accidents frequent. Keke can claim to be among the luckiest, because although he's had at least five major shunts, he has never been seriously injured. He does not remember them all; he probably does not wish to. The first was at Hockenheim in September 1974 and is memorably recorded by photograph. On that occasion, it was a last-lap battle and Keke's wheel caught Peter Scharman's and the resulting somersault could have been fatal. Luckily, he walked away intact.

In 1976, he had two major accidents in succession: one again at Hockenheim and another at Thruxton. The first was again the result of another of the frenzied charges that marked his beginnings in the sport: he hit another car and flew fifteen yards through the air, again escaping untouched.

I had had problems with the accelerator from the start of the race at Hockenheim; it kept sticking on me and that's what caused the accident. It's not worth talking about, except that I learned that you don't win races unless you arrive at the finish line.

The same thing occurred a week later at Thruxton. The throttle stuck and Keke went head on into the Armco.

Considering the force of the accident, I didn't really suffer too much. I couldn't walk afterwards; but if my Toj hadn't been so well built, there's every chance I would have lost my feet. The car was shortened by a yard.

His accident in a Can-Am at Laguna Seca in 1979 was the most serious of the three. It is described elsewhere (see p. 24–5). The results of these serious accidents were to mark him for the rest of his career.

The Atlantic accident was the lucky one. The Atlantic is still a pretty light car and although my knees were pushed right up into the instrument panel, my legs were destroyed and I had to go to hospital, I escaped with far fewer injuries than might have been expected. At the hospital, they said they could find nothing seriously wrong, but I had to be taken back two hours later because I didn't know who I was. I went back home to Germany on the next plane. The problem is that though I've never broken any major bones, I've smashed my heels and the lower part of my legs three times now. The result is that I'm often wrong-footed and less agile than I ought to be. My feet and ankles have become my weak point and sometimes give me pain; it comes and goes. I may look fit and healthy, but if I can't push on the brake or the throttle, then I'm in trouble. If I can't push hard on the brake, I may dance like a butterfly but I'm out.

I have another problem with my foot. It didn't really bother me until I began at Williams; ever since then it's troubled me. It hurt a lot in 1982 when I had a really fierce season of testing. In 1983 it wasn't so bad because, thanks to refuelling, we raced mostly on half-tanks, which reduced the weight of the car. But in 1984 it cropped up again: if you brake with full tanks in a turbo, there's no way you're not going to feel it. Luckily I seem to have found a cure to that now.

As for the accidents themselves, I'm philosophical about them. They are just part of the profession. One of the worst is when a throttle sticks. Then there's nothing you can do but pray and take what evasive action you can, at least try to get the car to hit sideways. Alan had a hook installed over his throttle pedal so that even if it stuck down, he could pull it back up, but that doesn't really help. The problem lies mostly in the engine.

Brakes can be just as bad. On my first ever Grand Prix, in South Africa, a brake came out of its caliper because it hadn't been properly fitted and I had another big one. I was going at 250 k.p.h. and I was only just able to head away from the wall into the catch fencing. The car took up a hundred yards of fencing and stopped with a catch-fence pole smashed into the chassis. Once again I was lucky.

Steering failures are so rare as to be negligible. A car can lose a wheel or break a suspension, but one of the reasons I went to Williams is that Patrick Head, like Gordon Murray, designs very safe cars. It's the throttle and the brakes that worry me, whoever designs the car.

Especially the throttle. All of a sudden you're coming up to a corner a hell of a lot faster than you should be. You lift off and nothing happens, but by then it's too late anyway. The automatic reaction is to brake even harder. You realize the car isn't stopping so you stand on the brakes. At which point you lock your front wheels and lose your steering. That prevents you from being able to change the angle of impact.

When you know it's going to happen, you just say, shit! You *know* it's going to hurt.

For me, it's always the head. It happens every time and it's a feeling you don't forget. The bang is a big one. That's what gives you the big pain. The rest of the pain comes afterwards. The impact is on your head: you black out, even if it's just for a second, because of the G-force. There's nothing you can do about it. All that business about relaxing like a drunk is impossible: there isn't time. The impact is taken by the safety harness, by your wrists on the steering wheel and by your feet.

That's why I use a heel bar. If you don't have one, it's almost certain you will break your ankles. Your foot will be on the brake and your ankle will go forward under the pedal. If you have one, you might get away with smashed heels.

Ankles and wrists, all the joints, are vulnerable. You can have them operated on, but there's no guarantee it will work.

7

First Steps into F1

1978 began with New Zealand again. Keke had barely been home for Christmas. He was in a Chevron B39 and the season started at Bay Park. Keke was on pole; third in the first session, he won the second. Five days later came the New Zealand Grand Prix at Pukekohe: he won the first leg, and the second after a spin which put him back to eleventh place. Eight days later, at Manfield, the result was a second place overall. The championship seemed in his hands. At Teretonga, despite a minute's penalty for a false start, Keke finished ninth in the first leg; the second leg was his. The last race was at Christchurch: Keke had to win the first session to be champion and succeeded; in the second, Bobby Rahal, who was his teammate, passed everyone on the inside and put Keke off. A second New Zealand championship.

Keke was more preoccupied with his F1 projects with Kojima in Japan. They were to come to nothing. A Japanese driver, Kunimitsu, tested the car after Keke and wrecked it. Kojima had a second car, but Willi Kauhsen couldn't get his act together.

Too bad! Thank God there were other irons in the fire. I had nothing to prove in New Zealand, but on the other hand I owed a lot to Fred Opert. Not to speak of the fact that my contract said I raced where Fred wanted. He thought he was doing me a favour. Frankly, I would have rather been in Europe where the contracts are signed for the coming year. That's where my career had to take off. But most of all I needed some rest.

Fortunately, as Keke says, other irons were in the fire. Eddie Cheever twice failed to qualify his Theodore as the 1978 season began in South America, and Teddy Yip invited Keke to take his place. As Keke saw it, his chances were mixed.

86

As has happened to other Finns, my career could have ended right here. But that's not the way I saw it. I was going to gain some experience in F1. There is no other way to acquire this experience but by driving and once I'd done that, no one could ever take it away from me. I wanted to see what F1 was like from the inside. I wanted to familiarize myself with that milieu. From F2 to F1 is a giant leap and I didn't expect much to start with. I didn't expect to win: frankly, I would have been happy to qualify! I got three days' practice and then three days' testing in Kyalami.

The car was originally designed by Ron Tauranac, then improved by every man in the street. It was really no more than a modified F2. Sid Taylor was team manager. Keke's first test in his F1 debut was no great success: the brakes gave at 250 k.p.h. and Keke ripped up a furlong of catch fencing, stopping with a catch-fence pole, as thick as a telephone pole, halfway into the cockpit. Otherwise, his debut was not without its encouragements.

The car was really not that bad. I kept up with the pace and was only a second behind Lauda in testing. Otherwise, the team was a disaster: everyone was busy fighting everyone else. There was no team spirit of any sort.

On his first outing in official practice, Keke was nineteenth; in the second session the Theodore's engine blew. During the race he had to stop on lap 15: his cockpit was full of fuel and he was nearly overcome by the fumes.

A choice was in the offing. Keke was still under contract with Fred Opert, but the races in Formula Atlantic were well spaced; that was no obstacle. He decided to stay faithful to Yip, having obtained a change of mechanics. After South Africa, the Daily Express *held a 'Race of Champions' at Silverstone. Only Ferrari and Wolf were absent and, after an arduous battle in the rain with ex-F1 champion Emerson Fittipaldi, Keke won: after everyone had gone off.*

A week later the F2 championship started. Keke was in a Chevron Hart B42. As the car had been built very slowly there was no time to test. Keke's letter to his father gives a vivid picture of what life is like in the lower echelons:

'The week after the Silverstone race has been nothing but a gnashing of teeth. There should have been daily tests, but no, the car isn't ready. I spent a week doing sweet nothing. I got into a violent argument with Fred: I told him championship contenders weren't built like that.'

As might have been expected, the F2 race at Thruxton gave a negative result: Keke started on the back row and the engine blew after four laps. A week later in Long Beach, with six pre-qualifiers, Keke failed to get his Theodore on the grid. Keke stayed in Long Beach for a Formula Atlantic race in an untested Chevron B45. During warm-up his engine lost half its power and then folded altogether: his race was over before it started. Hockenheim was next. It was the Jim Clark Memorial Race and the second leg of the European F2 championship. Second on the grid in the Chevron B42, his rear wing broke loose and then his left front tyre deflated. He was twelfth in the first leg and eighth overall.

I didn't really feel at home in Hockenheim; it's not a demanding circuit and power is all. In that respect we couldn't touch the BMW engines. Fred brought thirty-four tyres from America, but they did us no good and I finally raced on European Goodyears. I don't think I've ever fought as hard for a twelfth place.

In this, the maddest year of his career, Keke flew back to Canada, to Westwood in Vancouver. Rain for the race and Keke won. Keke hurried back to Europe to test the Theodore and then raced at the Nürburgring in F2. Despite a damaged nose, Keke finished second behind Alex Ribeiro. He was now fourth in the F2 championship, even with Eddie Cheever. Back in F1 for Belgium, Keke managed to qualify the Theodore for official practice, but was finally eliminated. It was time for Keke to reflect on his situation, which he does again in a letter to his father:

'You don't understand the situation. I have no reason to complain. True, I am in a mediocre team, but the truth is that I am part of an F1 team and that's where I had to start. In F2, my team is good, and don't forget I'm drawing two salaries. You shouldn't forget that I'm a professional and I have to earn my living. Even ordinary work is better than no work at all. Those who complain about my poor results in F1 don't look farther than their own noses. They see only today. I see much farther ahead. I am building my future in this bizarre job. There are ups and downs in every job. I don't think I've made any major errors to date: all you need is that the ups exceed the downs. I want to go up the ladder step by step by my own talents and my reputation as a pro. My progress is slow, slower than that of a lot of other drivers. I should have been where I am now some years ago, but I'm satisfied with things as they are.'

F2 at Mugello was next. Keke was beginning to feel the pressure and the exhaustion of racing week in and week out and changing cars all the time. Even his renowned capacity for sleep didn't seem to rest him enough. He was finding it hard to concentrate and showed signs of tension and irritability. Twice in practice he went off the track. Ninth on the grid, his Hart engine gave up the ghost.

Once again, Keke had second thoughts about staying with Theodore. This time Yip promised him a new car. But attempts to obtain one from team Arrows failed and Keke was eliminated at Jarama in Spain in the old one. The same weekend he rushed off to an F2 race at Vallelunga. There, Cheever blocked him for lap after lap, the rest of the field grew impatient and Gabbiani, having had enough of it, pushed Keke into the Armco. Six demoralizing weeks.

Keke sought refuge in Quebec; depressed and tired, he caught a cold and raced with a high fever. It resulted in his first victory for some time. He regained his confidence. Anderstorp in Sweden followed; so did all the old problems with the Theodore. None of the promises were kept and Keke was set free. Gunther Schmid of ATS had long wanted Keke as his number two behind Jochen Mass. Keke was doubtful, but content.

'The ATS is not a very quick car. I wonder whether it's the car or the driver. Without even getting into the car, I start practice. I've raced here before in a Super Vee, but the difference between Super Vee and F1 is great. Anyway, this contract is a one-off. Theodore has promised a new car for France. A new car: there aren't any! They're going to buy a last year's model: probably the Wolf with which Jody Scheckter finished second last season. It has to be better than an overweight Theodore.'

Still at Anderstorp, however, Keke finished fifteenth, many laps behind Niki Lauda. None the less, it was the first time ever that a Finnish driver had crossed the finish line in an F1 car! As he wrote his father:

'I'd rather be by a Finnish lake in a sauna by the water with a glass of iced beer, hearing nothing but wild duck flying overhead. I dream of such things in the mess in which I live. To do three different series simultaneously is too much: a race every weekend and testing in between! And then there's next season. I would rather not sign with Theodore, but ATS is no real solution either. As for F2, I feel I've outgrown it. None the less, I'm optimistic. Curious as it may seem, I've succeeded this year in stabilizing my position in the driver market. I'm not really interested in making my reputation in America; Europe is the heart of auto sport.'

Back to Donington for the next F2 race: Keke won the first leg and came fourth in the second. Some progress at last. Meanwhile, Teddy Yip had bought two Wolf cars, and the day after Donington Keke was off testing them in Hockenheim. His times were excellent. The only problem was tyres: only the big teams get the best. In France, he raced again for ATS. Keke barely qualified and finished sixteenth: the ATS situation was doubtful – no points meant no FOCA (Formula One Constructors Association) membership, no FOCA membership meant added expense.

At Lime Rock in the United States, Keke was placed sixth on the grid; he finished fourth and headed the Formula Atlantic championship. Fred Opert and Keke decided to concentrate on Formula Atlantic and relegate F2 to second place. But only three days after Lime Rock Keke put in a last F2 race at Nogaro. He failed to finish. It was time for him to concentrate on the British Grand Prix at Brands with the new Wolf cars. Further contretemps. The organizers had not accepted Teddy Yip's entry; it was the last reserve car. Extremely tense and upset, Keke went to ATS where there was a place free due to Jarier's illness. It had been promised to Vittorio Brambilla, but Keke managed to get the job. He was twenty-second on the grid but by some miracle ATS had obtained first-class tyres. He raced splendidly and reached fourth place with only Lauda, Reutemann and Watson ahead of him; but the rear axle broke and Keke was forced to retire.

He had just enough time to change his clothes and fly to Elkhart Lake.

In the race, his engine went off and he only finished seventh, dropping to second place in the championship. Then it was back to Hockenheim where he made his debut with the Wolf car. Nineteenth on the grid and despite breaking his front wing in a shunt with Tambay, he finished tenth: without the shunt, he might have been up among the leaders. Again, into a plane, this time to Hamilton. There was so much delay installing crash barriers that the race finished at nine at night: Keke had done two laps less than the required sixty and only half points were awarded; but he won the race.

Austria was next and Keke had to conclude practice in his spare; on the Friday he failed to qualify. On the Saturday it rained and Keke was the only driver to improve his time, just ekeing out a twenty-fifth place on the grid. Rain fell again seven laps into the race while Keke was climbing quickly through the pack to eighth place. A new start was ordered. His gearbox went and he drove on only second and sixth gears. In the circumstances, a tenth place was notable.

'The market is already in full swing. The stars have their drives. Now it's our turn. I think I have some chance. ATS and Theodore are both fairly sure, but I've made the rounds of several other teams. This has been my year of apprenticeship in F1 and it should be enough; if I don't get a decent car, I'll race in America. The pay is better and at least I'll get competitive equipment.'

Zandvoort, and Keke just made it, but in the race he shunted with Jody Scheckter: he took a ride through the air but managed to struggle on. But on lap 21 the throttle jammed and he went off. Another escape. Faced with so many disappointments, Teddy Yip announced he won't race in the United States and Canada.

'I understand his attitude. The car is not competitive and financially the odds are stacked against him. As for me, I'm going to be on the dole if I don't get a drive for next year.'

Monza was the last nail in the Theodore's coffin. Keke was eliminated with a dud engine. But Monza is like an Oriental bazaar; Keke was now a saleable product and the balance sheet was satisfactory: two Grands Prix for ATS, two F2 races for Fred Opert, the Macao Grand Prix in

Formula Atlantic and finally an F2 race in Japan. It wasn't enough. He wanted an F1 drive for 1979, and Monza became a place of tragedy with the death of Keke's old friend Ronnie Peterson.

The rest of 1978 Keke was far from Europe. He was fifth in F2 and in America now faced the last race in Formula Atlantic: at Montreal. The track, on the Ile Notre Dame, was brand new and Keke was the first F1 driver to go out on it. He finished only thirteenth after a spark-plug failure, but just retained his second place in the championship. From Montreal, Keke drove south to Watkins Glen with Fred Opert. Nothing. Keke retired with a broken gear lever while lying tenth. Still no points for ATS.

Then a holiday; then Argentina and F2: ninth in Mendoza and again in Buenos Aires. Macao. A retirement.

'I can't afford to rest and yet I am exhausted. I've travelled so much that I've lost track of whether it's night or day. And yet I must go into the marketplace. I must find some F1 work for next year. There are drives in the lesser teams, and not only are their cars uncompetitive, but their finances are just as weak. F1 takes so much money these days that one is better off not getting involved with a team unless it has guaranteed money for a whole year. To make matters worse, there are plenty of good F2 drivers around who are ready and able to bring their own money into a team. I have only one weapon: my professional skill. John Hogan at Marlboro is willing to give advice and I am grateful.'

For the time being nothing. Then, on his birthday, a call from Carl Haas in America: the Can-Am drive is his. Keke was overjoyed. Can-Am does not conflict with F1 and at least he had a job. Besides, the other three candidates for the Haas drive were Mass, Depailler and Jarier. Keke thought it a sign of his worth. He flew to Chicago and signed. Then it all turned to dust. As the year ended, Haas said he wanted another driver. Behind the scenes was Jackie Stewart: he apparently told Haas Keke was not a good enough driver. Haas gave as his reason that his sponsors didn't want Keke. Keke had never been so angry. Nor would he ever forget, or forgive.

As for the year? Thirty-eight races, twelve placings and an equal number of retirements, plus five non-qualifications. Number one in Formula

Pacific, number two in Formula Atlantic, number five in F2. But, more important than all else, fifteen races in F1.

Qualifying

There is a widespread feeling inside the sport that qualifying has become too dangerous and needs to be controlled. As it is, qualifying has two serious defects: first, it distorts the grid and in no way reflects the race result; second, it sends twenty-six drivers out at maximum speed for two hours on narrow and inadequate circuits to set the fastest time under the worst possible conditions for safety. Keke doesn't want qualifying tampered with. He is in his usual minority position.

How can anyone tell me what is the most dangerous part of my life unless he tries it out himself? I understand there are a number of drivers who support a proposal to make the official qualifying time an average of the five best laps in practice rather than one flying lap. At present I know how to find the space, the gap, to do one fast lap; how would I ever find the space to do five fast laps? Five *consecutive* laps?

It's not going to improve the tyre situation or the engine situation, which is what makes qualifying so unsatisfying at present. Even if there were only one manufacturer supplying tyres in F1, there would still be teams who would find a way to get more out of those tyres and others who would adjust their engines accordingly.

The way it is now, we at least know the rules of the game. Give me any kind of rubber and I'll get one fast lap out of it. That one quick lap is one of the deep thrills and satisfactions of F1: why tamper with it?

I know all the arguments about qualifying. They came to the fore after Gilles was killed at Zolder. What happened to Gilles was one accident too many, but the fact is we don't have that many accidents in qualifying. I don't hear anyone suggesting that we ban the race because occasionally someone does go off. It's all part of the profession.

You can't eliminate qualifying altogether. You can't draw straws from a hat. I like the European way of looking at culture and history rather than the American. Part of the history of F1 is qualifying, so, unless it can be improved, don't fiddle with it. Let's keep things as they are. F1 has too many changes in it anyway.

There are all sorts of possibilities. You can't qualify one by one because conditions will never be the same for two drivers. You could have a rating system, as they do in downhill skiing. The first three in the championship go out at the same time, the next three and so on. I'd quite like that.

Alternatively, we could start twenty-six abreast, of course. But that would cause a hell of a mess at the first corner.

No matter what sort of solution you come up with, there are still going to be fast laps and there's still going to be one man faster than the rest.

It's not just that I like the way we qualify now. That would be to oversimplify. What I like is the pressure it puts on me. I like the intense concentration and the determination it requires. I like to have to put the best of myself into just one lap.

I prepare myself mentally for that one lap, so that when the word is go, I really go. It's like letting all the horses loose from the box. Bang! It's on! It's solid action for one lap. All you need is that your reactions be super-quick, because that's what the lap is.

There is a technique to it which is quite different from race technique: obviously, because you're only doing a one-off. Much depends on the weather. If the weather is stable, I don't go out in the first minute when most drivers are out. Each of us has only two sets of qualifiers and there's plenty of time: why rush? At Williams we often use one hard set of tyres and one soft; that's a compromise which will hurt you in qualifying, but theoretically it should help you for the race. If I have two sets of super-softs, then I wait. I use the first set fifteen or twenty minutes in practice and the next set immediately afterwards if the track is empty; if it isn't, I wait a few minutes and see what the situation is on the track. A great deal depends on finding a good slot and not going out after all the engines qualifying have blown their oil onto the track.

After that, everything depends on the rubber. You have to get the feel of your tyres very quickly. Do you scuff it in for one lap or more? How hard do you scuff it in, how fast do you go? What you're looking for is the optimum temperature. That depends on the tyre. If you have a very soft tyre and you're using two laps to scuff it in, then you can overdo it and it'll get too hot before your real lap begins: in which case it will go off before you finish that lap.

You really need feel. Ideally, the tyre will come in perfectly on the first corner of the lap and just be going off on the last. It's also on that warming-up lap that you have to find your slot. And there are circuits, like South Africa, where you have no idea who's just gone into the pits or who is just coming out. It's never easy. Unfortunately, all too often you're just coming into your fast lap when you see someone going slowly in front of you, someone who may not be paying attention. Then you have to think quickly. Is this someone who is going to leave you a clear line? Can you be sure he's seen you? If he hasn't, you stand on the brake.

The only thing you know is what everyone else has done by way of a time. When you go out you know roughly what you have to do. You also know just how short one lap is and how few chances you've got of doing it. That's the challenge. Naturally, everyone else is thinking the same thing.

Traffic is a nuisance, but it's my job to protect myself from traffic. I curse anyone who gets in my way. I curse anyone who makes me slow down. That's normal: everything I have to offer in terms of speed and technique is being put into this one lap. But I have sense enough to back off if I have to.

That's my judgement. I'm hired for that as well as my speed. If you are a highly qualified racing driver and you have spent ten to fifteen years racing professionally, you know what you can and can't do.

Part of me is a whip which says, 'go!' Another part is a rein which says, 'Hold on!'

The fast lap is a very intense moment. The rewards are internal. It is one of those beautifully simple things in life which you can appreciate to the full because at the end of it you have a result, a time.

In effect, however, with the advent of turbos, qualifying has been totally devalued. It no longer really means anything. We now have two separate events, qualifying and racing. For Cosworth cars, though, it wasn't two separate events. It was as it always was: a reflection of your performance, of how good your chassis is, how good your engine, how good your driver is on a quick lap. In the race the only difference from qualifying used to be more weight and a harder tyre: just like everyone else. Back in the days where there were only Cosworths, the fastest six usually produced the winner of the race.

Now, qualifying reflects nothing at all. If you use the same engine as your race engine, you still have a turbo boost, which in effect means you have two different engines – and with some teams, it's literally two different engines – and as you don't have to worry about fuel consumption in qualifying, a turn-up of the boost will produce a quick time. Even your chassis performs completely differently when a few turns on the boost are added. So, the only element common to qualifying and to the race is the driver, and the driver by himself isn't a big enough factor to out-weigh all the others. Therefore qualifying gives you little indication of a race situation. You don't really know the power the car can offer you when you're racing heavy on full tanks, when the wick's been turned down and you're on hard tyres. It's no longer practice; it's a separate race.

Gears

One of the most constant and unremitting tasks a driver performs in the car is the gear-change; as Keke says, he does this somewhere between 1500 – 2500 times in a race. That is a lot of wear: on the gears and on the driver.

Though F1 gears are much more precise than those on road cars, they are hard work: any repetitive action puts a strain on the hand, on the brain. If you watch a driver's hand on the gear lever, it looks like an action of no consequence at all. It's very quick, so quick as to be imperceptible. But to the driver it is always too slow, particularly on turbo cars, where each time you shift you lose pressure.

As I've grown used to turbos, I find I don't use the clutch at all for the higher gears. I just let the throttle fall back half or three-quarters and shift. Other drivers use the clutch and don't lift the throttle at all. The difference between the two techniques is that my engine won't blow up and theirs have a good chance of doing

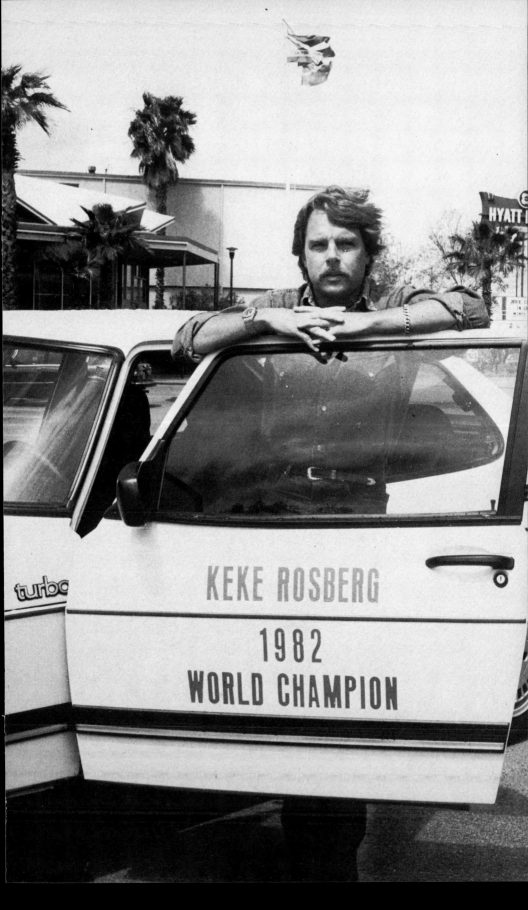

Above   At Donnington in F2

Left   1977 – Keke was in F2 then with Fred Opert

Below   The F2 Chevron, 1977

eke at Brands Hatch for ATS, 1978

the Theodore at Silverstone, 1978 – Keke's first F1 win

The Wolf crew at Watkins Glen, 1979. Peter Warr is second from left

In the Wolf car at Zeltweg in 1979

Niki – the old fox himself

Alan Jones, now back from retirement

Teddy Yip, owner of the Theodore team

John Watson at the British Grand Prix, 1982

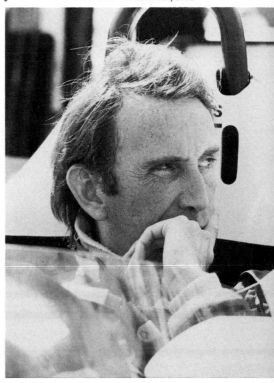

Sometimes reflective, as here in 1982 …

Frank Williams – 1983 gave much food for thought

… Sometimes jovial, as here in hot Brazil, 1983

Keke's cars, 1983 version

The first Keke plane ... A Learjet followed

The famous Balestre finger wags, here at Jacques Laffite

Keke looks like he is reassuring Frank Williams

Elio de Angelis and Nigel Mansell

Keke and manager Ortwin Podlech

With Frank Williams and engineer Neal Oately

Detriot, 1983 – things had started to slip

Dallas, 1984 – Keke's third victory

The rainiest race – Monaco, 1984

Keke's wife, Sina

so. It's not that they use the clutch, it's because they keep full throttle; that lets the engine fly over the limit without drive.

The shift has its own technique. It's quick, but it requires not a little shove and strength. You have to apply the right amount of power to it; it has to be very precise; the gear has to engage. Depending on the set-up, there can be a little bit of resistance in the gear-shift. If there is a long gap between gear ratios, it can be stiff and unyielding; if the gear ratios are close, it just goes click, click.

Every engine needs different gear ratios for different circuits: that's one of the elementary things you learn early on. Unlike road cars, F1 gears are not compromises; they are designed to attack.

Naturally, as cars get lighter from using up their fuel, you may have to adapt your gear-changes. Sometimes when you have to differentiate between full tanks and near-empty tanks you find you are between two gears. But I am aware of that beforehand. I've thought about it long before the race: should I change my gear ratios because I'm going to have that problem? Is the difference big enough to be critical? Take Spa, for instance, where you go down the hill and then up again towards the esses. At first I was doing it in fourth and hitting the top of the hill in fifth, but as soon as the race was a third gone, I did it all in fifth, down and up. I was pretty quick.

Every track also requires you to use your gears differently. If you have 1000 r.p.m. between two gears, it is very easy to nurse those gears because the distance between them is small. As soon as you have a bigger gap between gears, say 2000 r.p.m., then you have to be extremely careful engaging the next gear or you can destroy the dog rings.

There's a big difference in the feel of the thing. It's something you feel right through the stick. You move the stick and hold your breath, hoping you won't hear the krr, krr . . .

Corners

One of the things those who follow motor racing watch for when it comes to driving technique is how a driver takes his corners. The theory is that the most economical, the most consistent, the most flawless is also the quickest per lap. It is easy, in fact, to see the difference between drivers, but is the difference always due to the driver? Or does much depend on the handling quality of the car, the choice of tyres or half a dozen other of the arcana of the sport?

Getting every lap smooth and right is very much a matter of how you corner. I have a lot of pride in driving through each corner in the same way, lap after lap. There is such a thing as a correct line, an apex, a braking point, an acceleration point. Naturally, you may not always be able to take it up; there could be another car in the way, there could be dust, oil and so on. But regularity is important. I don't think of 'taking' a corner; I think of challenging it. I like to think I am challenging a corner every time I go through it. I am attacking it.

Every corner is absolutely different and every corner has a different exit. How I attack a corner has more to do with what comes after it than with the corner itself and the fifty yards of braking that lead into it. In fact, the corner itself is unimportant. What is important is your exit speed into the straight that follows.

Most corners are decided after you've turned your car or just as you do so, depending on the camber of the track, the surface, the handling of your car – watch out if they've just laid a new patch of asphalt somewhere, that means bumps. All that is instinctive. It's happening too fast for anyone to have a real plan.

Gears are vital, too. You have to be in the right gear coming into the corner so that you come out of it on suitable revs and are able to accelerate before your next shift up. You certainly don't want to shift as you're cornering because that will slow you down. Nor do you want to come out of it running out of revs.

If you have a series of corners to face, you always have to compromise in some way: you have to leave the first corner so as you can enter the second one right.

Corners are the heart of the matter. They exist to slow you down. The quickest driver is the one who solves them in such fashion that they take the least possible time. That's why each race is preceded by five hours of practice. I can see every corner of every track I've ever raced on in my mind. Even if I can't do them all perfectly every time, I know them as well as I know my car.

Corners have their own character. The Monaco corners, particularly the Casino, are very individual. The only thing I don't like at Monaco is the fast chicane. It doesn't give you time to know exactly where your car is and thus avoid hitting the kerbs. But at least it's not dull. Detroit is. I don't seem to be able to get the feel of it: most of the stuff is 90 degrees around the block, 50 yards and then another 90 degrees. After a bad first year, they've improved the circuit a lot. They've done a great job, but I just can't get excited about it.

I suppose I like challenges. The Casino is a real challenge. It's a funny corner: it starts with the camber going in and then the camber turns the other way. If you don't get your nose in tight enough, you never will. If you enter too fast along the wrong side of the road for the tight right-hander you've really blown the combination. You should never go more than halfway out and come out of the left-hander really tight on the left – I mean really tight, maybe two inches off the Armco – so that you're able to brake while still cornering. The right-hander that follows is vital because it leads into the straight. It's very tricky too, because it drops off; if you enter it wrong, from the right side, the inside, the brow makes it absolutely impossible for you to negotiate the corner. It's one of those curves that you have to get dead right: tight, with a late apex so that when the car drops over the brow you have plenty of room – you need the room because when you accelerate the car will move over to the left.

Needless to say, the perfect corner rarely exists. There is always a very good chance of not finding yourself alone. That means one of two things: either you're in a position where you might be able to overtake someone, or someone else is in a position to overtake you. Thus, when you enter a corner you have to have a very clear idea of where everyone is. That's fairly automatic because your mind is working all the time clocking up who is moving up on you in the straight before the corner. You should know where they are and not be caught napping.

If the perfect corner doesn't exist, there is no chicane that is anything other than diabolical. A chicane exists because it is cheaper for circuit-owners to put in a first- or second-gear corner than it is to build one that can be driven through at speed. It costs less: less tarmac, less space, less run-off, less Armco. Drivers may have invented them   because the tracks were getting faster than the drivers could handle – but by and large they have destroyed racing and destroyed more cars than you could count. Aqua Minerale at Imola, chicanes at Zandvoort, Zolder, Monza, Monte Carlo, Silverstone – there you only think whether your car's going to hit the kerb or not.

Chicanes deny your driving skill; it's like driving through a hole. No one's ever asked me my opinion. Why should they? I'm just the guy who has to drive through these poles. I've seen some drivers insisting on them. Chicanes are simply the antithesis of driving; they are obstacles; they are cheap, that's why they exist.

Overtaking

If you're about to be overtaken, the action you take depends on a lot of things. Maybe you don't know enough about the man behind you; you can't be sure what he's going to try. Or maybe it's someone you know is quicker than you, in which case you know that, sooner or later, he's going to overtake you, so why wouldn't this be as good a place as any to let him by?

The decision you take is a function of your personality. Unless, of course, you're being lapped. I would never hold anyone back if I was being lapped. The only exception would be if I was having a fight with someone, and even then it wouldn't be for long. Say I'm in third place, fighting it out with the second-place man and I've worked hard for ten or fifteen laps pulling him in. I've got the leader coming up on me, but he's in no hurry to lap me, so why should I let him by and destroy the good work I've done? Then I say, 'OK, you'll find your place in front of me soon enough; I need to concentrate on the man in front of me.' But if the lead driver shows me clearly that he's desperate to get by, then I let him by. I wouldn't want to risk having a desperate driver behind me while I have to keep my eye on the man in front. I can usually tell: if he comes right up behind me several times, I know, and that's going to slow me up anyway. Better to let him go by and tow behind him to get back to my immediate rival.

The calculations are infinite. If I have a leader in front of me, I'm second and there's a third man pushing me hard, what I do really depends on what stage of the race we're in: on the first lap, let him by; if it's the last lap, then he's going to have to work to get past me. It also depends on how hard he's trying, how much quicker he is than I am, and *where* he's quicker.

Risk

All drivers live with, and deny, risk. It is such common stuff in their lives, like having enough pennies in your pocket, that often they hardly think of it. Above all, they do not like to talk of it. The man who is afraid of the risks he takes does not become a driver: that is an axiom. Yet, as it is something they live with every time they go out in a car, some of the silence on the subject is the result of familiarity. It is their job: as a fireman's is to put out fires. The dread is familiar. Familiar to the point of being suppressed.

But, being intelligent human beings, drivers also reach an accommodation with risk, with the possibility – or some would say the probability – of injury and death. The way they do this is by persuading themselves that, being highly trained in their craft, they can control those forces which could lead to injury. In other words, they reduce the element of chance.

It is true that there are drivers who are deliberate seekers after death. I have known them. Patrick Depailler once said to me that he did not expect to live beyond his racing days. It is the kind of remark that is really a self-fulfilling prediction. He did not. I hold that his not doing so was deliberate. Gilles Villeneuve was another. He lived a high song, a long aria and, I suspect, knew it would end as it did. And, furthermore, wanted it to end that way. Of him and of others like him you could say that they would rather go in the exercise of their profession than live out the drab life which inevitably follows on such peaks of excitement.

Fortunately, there are not very many such drivers. The vast majority do not want injury, nor to die. The fact that they may is a condition of their profession.

I know that some people think of me as a brave racing driver. It is a matter of what you mean by the word 'brave'. There are brave men and brave men. There is brave and smart, brave and safe, brave and foolhardy. I raced a lot against Gilles Villeneuve in Formula Atlantic. I think we were both brave and determined. We banged wheels with each other because nothing was more important to either of us than winning. Gilles was a brave man and never changed until the day he died. I think I'm still brave, but I don't now take the risks I used to take in those days.

I will go this far: the point at which I think something is risky is probably farther down the road with me than with most drivers. It's like a curve: one man's risk is another man's judgement that no risk is involved. The question is, where does judgement end and risk begin? What is normal in racing, and what is dangerous? Every driver feels that point to be in an entirely different place.

Put it another way, you probably cannot be a first-class driver without having your limits on risk set fairly high. But equally, you cannot be a first-class driver unless your awareness of risk is equally high. I have a high threshold for risk. Everybody drives to some limit.

People think that when a risk arises perhaps the driver doesn't have time to perceive it. Maybe he is so engaged in whatever he is doing that the moment of perception is past before he sees it as a risk. The truth is, you *always* have enough time to consider a risk. That's how instinctive driving is.

Take cornering. I love to commit myself to a corner. But I have to consider where the risk starts. I don't commit myself if I think I'm going to fly off. Most drivers don't think of commitment as risk. But there's a fine line that separates commitment from risk. All drivers know about that line, just as they know the risks are there.

If you've been out of a car for a while, you lose the instinct a bit. You lose your sense of speed; consequently you have to adjust to that. The aim is to go through the corner as quickly as possible, but you don't go quickly if you think you're taking a risk. So what you do is adjust bit by bit, lap by lap: you adjust the speed and the risk. You turn the screw up. Sometimes it comes easily. Sometimes you positively like doing it.

It might seem that I like to approach the threshold of risk. I think of it as a game in the mind and most drivers don't think of that sort of commitment as a risk. It is a struggle against a mental impediment, a sort of risk barrier. It's your mind that calculates the risk, not your body, which might suffer the consequences if you get it wrong.

You can feel cold fear. I've felt it. But I don't think you get to the point where you're trying to banish the fear. You don't think as far as the fear. You stop short of that and reduce it to a risk.

Fear is something you feel only when you reach the point where you are about to lose control. At that point you have no alternative but to control that fear. You have no choice. Your life depends on it. And you do control that fear. How? You have to stop your hands trembling and your heart pounding. They are things you get used to, but you never manage to control them completely. But if you want to get driving fast again, it takes a microsecond or two. You've been on the edge.

Taking risks becomes a habit. When I started out, I thought travelling was the biggest risk I took. Nothing scared me more than the taxi drivers in Buenos Aires. I still think that way. On the roads I'm no better a driver than anyone else. I can't concentrate on it as I can in a racing car. It's like flying: the most dangerous pilot is the one who thinks he can fly and who doesn't concentrate, concentrate all the time. The risks are fewer in flying, but in travel? The more travelling you do, the more likely you are to be involved in some disaster. I drive a hundred days a year. The other 250 days strike me as presenting the greater risk.

I had a big crash in a road car two years ago. I walked away from it with my suitcases, not even looking to see what had happened. For fifteen seconds after the crash I was completely calm. Then I thought, What happens now? And my conscious mind took over again: get a tow-truck and get it organized.

In racing you take a different view of safety, or the risks involved. Football, bike races, all sports are dangerous. None, you say, like motor sport. But that is a calculated risk. The calculation is based on yourself, for there is only one man who can protect you from risk, and that's yourself.

I'm talking about professionals acting as professionals, men saying: this car is drivable; this problem is going to be dangerous;

103

racing against so-and-so in these conditions is stupid. I'm talking about the use of judgement. Judgement is what protects you.

I run a special risk, because I am made in such a way that I only really enjoy racing on the limit. I have to dampen that enjoyment by using my brain; I have to be conscious that I sometimes push too hard and say to myself, 'A little less joy, Keke, a little more prudence, a little more judgement.' It's hard to control myself in that way. But to be at the limit too often is crazy.

When you've raced as long as I have you get more and more cautious. I've made mistakes: anyone who lives on a very fine limit as I do is bound to make mistakes. You just have to make sure that when you make a mistake you're still thinking of protecting yourself so that the mistake doesn't turn out to be a bad one. Try not to get quite so close to that limit, because when the mistake comes and you're too close to the limit, there's no longer anything you can do about the mistake.

I know the public thinks otherwise. The public thinks I drive with my balls. I live very strongly within my limits.

Fortunately, that image – of being totally self-destructive – does me no harm. I couldn't have a better one. But it's totally wrong.

Starts

To the spectator at the circuit – if he's lucky or rich enough to have access to the start–finish line – or to the television viewer, the start is the moment of maximum excitement: twenty-six engines revving up, twenty-six drivers ready to go, the likelihood of at least a spill or two, the noise, the sudden release. As Alan Jones pointed out, from inside the cockpit of an F1 car the view is very different. To Alan it looked as wide and straightforward as a motorway. To Keke it is a point of maximum concentration. His opening description is typical: a driver's eye view of one of the sixteen starts he makes in a season.

I had my eye on a spot between the two Ferraris ahead of me on the grid, so when the light went green I pointed my car straight up the arse of one Ferrari and when I lifted the clutch I got the slide so that my tail drifted out to the right as I wanted. Then I turned my wheel the other way and went from the right into a slide to the left, which I had to correct to get between them. I found I'd overcorrected because I had a huge wheel spin. The problem is, the whole grid turns immediately. I should have paid no attention to that and pointed my car straight into the slot. Had I done so, I would have got through instead of knocking Arnoux's front wheel. If I'd just gone straight into the slot, I'd have missed some slides; you get them if your car goes sideways: you lose grip. Good start.

It sounds laconic, but there's a huge amount to think about in those five to ten seconds after the warm-up lap.

To start with, there are so many things that can go wrong. You can have too few revs in the engine, in which case you're not making a very fast start; or you can have too many revs, in which case you have too much wheel spin; no traction; cook the clutch; forget the race. If you have a short first gear you hit the limit too soon before you can shift into second. If you have a long first gear, you can cook the clutch or stall the engine. There's a lot that can go wrong, especially nowadays when the real commander of the ship is a computer.

Even your position – you can line up 'anywhere' or in 'any way' inside your marked slot – is important. If you're on pole at Brands Hatch, for instance, you don't put your car straight; you put it three fifths into the wall and look as odd as hell. But if you've put your car straight, your tail comes out immediately as you drop down the hill. So you face your car downhill beforehand, facing the wall, and that gives you a perfect start.

That's not the sort of stuff you learn in driving school. It's something you figure out for yourself. You know your car's going to go sideways down a hill, so you face it downhill. That's Brands Hatch. Most tracks are fairly level and that's why you get the car pointing straight, because that way you get better traction. You still have to consider water puddles that have leaked out of engines, and dust. Most circuits have a specific starting line.

The tension at the start comes in part from the waiting, in part from thinking of all the things that can go wrong, in part from just tightening up watching for a light to change. I think I'm a good starter, but I've had to recognize that with a turbo it's become more difficult. With a turbo you have to get your wheels spinning or else you'll stall; at the same time, you can't slip the clutch too much because it gives you a hell of a lot more power and the car is heavier than an aspirated car used to be. You can slip it a little, but you have to be very careful and keep the revs high enough so that you're in the turbo range: that's somewhere between 9000 and 11,000 revs, a point at which it's very hard to keep the revs constant, because that's a lot of power for an engine that's not connected to anything. The revs don't have to drop a lot when you come up with the clutch: bang, end of story.

I used to enjoy the starts in 1983 with the Cosworth because you really couldn't blow a start if you did everything exactly as you were supposed to. It was less fun in 1984 because with the turbo you can blow the start even if you're doing everything absolutely by the book.

It isn't so much that I like the start better than any other part of the race; it's that the start is when the action begins and action is what I like. It puts an end to all the preparation that's been going on for weeks and seems like for ever, preparing the car, improving the car, checking the car. When you crawl into your box at the start, all that's behind you. You don't even worry about how the car's going to handle; at least you're going to know about that soon enough, in the second phase of the first lap. That's when you start worrying about the handling.

Starting in the rain is another question. There's no real problem if you're at the front or can get in front: that determines whether you've got any visibility. In a wet start, the action is all packed into the first fifty yards or so; then the spray comes up, the rear wings start throwing it up and that's the end of it. By then you'd better have found your slot, unless the track is wide enough and you can find a slot to one side or another of the cars in front of you. But if you're at the back, there is no such slot: just a lot of drivers looking for one. The wise thing to do is to slow down, because in a wet start it doesn't matter how slow you are, all the cars are sitting there waiting for you at the first corner, where the whole game stops because no one can see a thing. The first man into the corner brakes 50 yards early, the next 75 yards too early, the third 100 yards too early and if you're way back you might as well lift off on the straight. I can tell you: you do – first because you can't see anything, and second because what's the hurry, you're not going to lose anything. You can only improve your position because you can get past all the people who've fallen off at the first corner. On the other hand, if you're first on the grid, then you've got a great chance. You can just pull away: you're the only man with a clear start.

After that, long before the first corner, you've got your slot in the queue and you keep to that slot unless there's someone behind you who's desperate. There always seems to be someone in the queue who thinks he's going to conquer the world on the first corner, and then you have to take evasive action. He's the sort of man you want to avoid.

Monza is a good example. You start towards the chicane at the end of the straight which narrows down towards it. Anyone who's out to conquer the world at the first chicane at Monza is someone you're going to bang wheels with. Even if you have to lose two or three places in avoiding him, that's not such a big deal.

Monza is a very tight circuit after the start, so there's doubly no reason for making a mistake. You build up a lot of speed at Monza, there is a long braking area and there always seems to be a would-be hero when you come up to the first corner. I tend to lose places in the chicane at Monza. Hockenheim is another good example. There, you come up to a 90-degree corner. If you are anywhere behind the second row on the grid, you select a shorter gear than you would at racing speed: if it's a second-gear corner, you go into it in first – there's always a lot of confusion there, it's a very low-speed corner – and that one-gear difference means you might be the one who's not going to bog his engine down when you come up to the long straight that follows. Half of them do: they go in like crazy, stir their gear-shift as if it were a cocktail-shaker and only then find there's no power to come out of the corner. The idea is to go in slowly and then boot it onto the straight. Normally you lose a place going into that corner because some hero goes by; you win it back coming out because all the heroes are sitting there fishing for a gear.

The tyres are still cold, so are the brakes, there's still dust on the track: two heroes at the same corner is bad news. But quite amusing if you're a gear lower down.

Then there are places like Zandvoort at Tarzan Corner where there's not much you can do: the queue goes in and the queue comes out. Unless there's another hero who finds a non-gritty part of the track on the outside. Even then, the whole queue goes past him on the inside.

I try not to fool around at the start. For instance, I've never tried anything on at the chicane in Monza. Unless you're second on the grid, there's no point. Even if you are there's no point, for the simple reason that there are always heroes willing to nip your slot. What I do is take a tight inside line so that no one can bang wheels with me. If I don't have a hero alongside, I move to the middle a bit to get a better line coming out, because by then it's too late for anyone to move to the inside of me. No one bangs from the outside.

It's like my brush with Tambay in Long Beach. You have to keep the inside covered. It's the driver on the inside who bangs; in this case it was I. At the end of the day, it doesn't matter whose fault it is; the results are the same and it's your race that's gone. If you're on the outside and someone's on the inside, it's your job to make sure he doesn't bang into you, as I did into him. There's no point in having a shunt and then saying it's his fault. There are two hours to go, and even if you lose two places on a first corner you're not going to be crying. Only in Monaco. Then you say, 'Shit!'

There's no special strategy after the start itself. Or at least I'm not conscious of any grand strategy until I'm some way into the race, the point at which I know whether I'm struggling or leading. Unless, of course, I'm on pole: in which case my tactic, having worked hard to earn that pole position, is to head off into the wild blue yonder.

Otherwise, the early part of the race, after I've found my niche in life, is the time to analyse everything that's going on. Mainly tyres, because I can probably handle the rest. A driver has a special feel for his tyres. How hard does he have to drive to get away from a pursuer or to catch up to someone in front? He has to consider the compound he's using. Is it marginal? Will it stand up? Especially in a hot race. You always push your car no harder than necessary.

Next I might consider the engine? How about the gearbox? And then a question that always underlies every other but is seldom conscious: how hard am I using myself? I only really think about that if I'm in the lead.

All these questions affect my strategy. And if something's wrong, the most I can do is lay off and drive the car as smoothly and as fast as possible under the circumstances. But no matter how badly the car is behaving, it's not in my nature to give up. Even if the race is gone, my instinct is still to go for it.

Pit stop

Stopping to change tyres and refuel was a feature of the 1983 season; refuelling was banned in 1984. It was admittedly dangerous; it was also spectacular. For the driver, though, it was hell.

Nothing was more frustrating. I would sit there counting seconds, just sitting there with the impression that nothing was going on except that time was going by, so that it eventually came to feel more like two months than twenty seconds. In fact, I was concentrating on a dozen things: trying to keep my engine running, keep my brakes on so that the mechanics could get the wheels on, thinking about the time I was losing and who was outside gaining on me, worrying about not cocking up my exit from the pits, hoping the brake fluid wouldn't boil over or the engine overheat. Only, while it's going on, you're so busy doing things to make sure nothing goes wrong that you don't have that much time to think: and then there's the blessed moment when the chief mechanic's hand goes up and you're back to your job. That's release and it's worth it.

8

Side Steps

*As his father says, Keke is two ways smart: he likes and knows business
and he talks to people. After what Keke saw as a Haas double-cross, Keke
went straight to Paul Newman and started negotiating. F1 was a bit
touchier. ATS were after him and Keke got Fred Opert into the team,
thinking they might make a go of it. But Keke was still undecided.*

One of the things I most wanted to do was beat Jacky Ickx in
Haas's Lola. I wanted to prove him wrong. As for F1, I thought
a year's apprenticeship might be enough, but no. I might have
been impatient, but I had to remember that for want of money
I was several years behind other drivers. I was getting older and
didn't have that much time left to reach the top.

*Keke got an offer from Ron Dennis, who was under pressure from ICI to
do two races in F2: Hockenheim and the Nürburgring. ICI was to
become Keke's major backer. At the same time ATS came back with an
offer of a contract for the year in F1. Fred Opert fed him inside information: the cars weren't ready, the team was rent by dissent. Paul Newman came up with a deal in Can-Am and in April 1979, rested, Keke
headed to Hockenheim in his March F2, a race which he won; at the
Nürburgring, in rain, his throttle jammed and Keke went off at high
speed: minor injuries and the car was wrecked. His only memory of that
race is his incredible pole-position qualifying time.*

*The Can-Am season started in Atlanta. His hand was still swollen
from the accident in Germany, but Keke managed second on the grid
behind Ickx. After eight laps Keke took Ickx and the victory. Two weeks
later the fight continued in Charlotte; there the organizers claimed that
Keke had overtaken the pace car and penalized him enough to put him
behind Ickx. More trouble at Mosport, a damaged wheel and later a spin.*

110

At Mid-Ohio Keke won pole position ahead of Alan Jones. Later Jones shoved him off, but Keke still managed to finish second. He was third in the championship.

The same weekend James Hunt decided to retire and there was a drive open at Wolf. Keke called team manager Peter Warr who said, 'I was just leaving for the airport with a contract!' It was the beginning of a long relation of mutual respect and the start of learning the F1 trade from someone who was good at it. Keke was as clear-headed as usual.

'The best James Hunt's been able to do in the car is eighth. If I do as well, all right; if I improve on that, I'll be in the points, so much the better. It ought to be possible. The whole team works well and Peter Warr is a real professional: at last I'm working with someone who knows his job. But I need some results. I have to look to next year. It's no help being a Finn. The sponsors are more and more important and they don't have enough going for them in Finland to make me an attractive proposition. My only asset is my driving.'

Renault won the race and Keke finished ninth after a spirited battle with Carlos Reutemann. Testing at Zeltweg preceded another transatlantic flight to Watkins Glen for the next Can-Am race, which he won. Keke now led the Can-Am table, four points ahead of Ickx. Back to Silverstone, where he was on the seventh row alongside Villeneuve and ahead of de Angelis. He was fifth in the race when he lost all fuel pressure; the pits couldn't remedy the fault and he retired. The Wolf designer, Harvey Postlethwaite, now at Ferrari, has him clearly: 'He's a bit like Jody Scheckter. Hunt was always satisfied with the way the car was set up, even if it was slow; Keke wants changes. He's a man out to get ahead and that will to win allows him to make up for his mistakes: it's that extra effort that gives him that extra speed. James had given up.'

Back in the United States, at Elkhart Lake, a pole position was followed by retirement. With a heavy cold and fever, Keke returned to Formula One. The new WR9 was ready. On the Friday at Hockenheim it had brake problems; on Saturday he just managed seventeenth in the new car. On race day, however, nothing worked: a dream start and then the oil pressure went. Walter Wolf was impatient; he talked of getting out. Peter Warr was depressed. Keke wrote to his father:

'This was the second time I've been frankly ashamed on a circuit. Imagine the despair when all you can do is sit in the car and watch the other cars go by. At least the engine gave out and I could quit. It wasn't that I was ill: the car just wouldn't go any faster. It's really odd: I had a good first race, an even better one at Silverstone even if I had to retire, now it's catastrophe time again. Year by year, what a driver can do with the car diminishes; it's the engineers who now dominate and not a one of them can tell you why a car is quick or slow. Even in testing, the driver has become less important. A new car is either fast or it isn't. It doesn't matter if the driver's called Niki or Keke. Take Lotus: if I'd been offered a drive there last year I'd have jumped to the skies; look at them this year. If a genius like Chapman knew the whys and wherefores of that, drivers like Andretti and Reutemann wouldn't be in the shit they're in now. Look at Niki: last year's triumphs are gone with the wind, yet he's no worse a driver than he was in 1978.'

Another retirement followed at the Österreichring and Keke was off to Minnesota; Ickx won and Keke spilled oil all over the track. Zandvoort raised his morale: eighth on the grid, he was among the leaders and had reached fourth place when his engine blew on the thirty-third lap. But Wolf was still talking of quitting and Keke was already looking to the following year. Can-Am at Trois Rivières was another failure when in the lead and Monza loomed: last on the grid and in the race, the Wolf held everyone up, it was so slow. Now panic set in at Wolf. Walter Wolf wanted to give up. If he decided to stay, Keke would stay, despite another offer from ATS. Keke was close to deciding that it might be better to race among the rich in the United States than among the deprived in F1. A sixth place at Imola in a non-championship race was small consolation. Next to last was Montreal, where Niki walked out during practice, saying he'd had enough. Keke was eliminated after an accident with a stuck skirt, another miraculous escape. At Watkins Glen, another failure. A year with Wolf and not a single point. Walter Wolf then sold his whole team to Emerson Fittipaldi. While Keke was still thinking about his future, which looked problematical – for Fittipaldi wanted a Brazilian as his number two – there remained two Can-Am races. At Laguna Seca he had a serious shunt which left him with broken ribs, a fractured wrist and severe concussion. He raced on the Sunday none the less, finishing eighth. In the last race, at Riverside, Keke was on pole; he spun off and retired, finishing fourth in the championship. Fittipaldi, however, was in the offing. Keke's hopes were high. After 1979, 1980 could only be better.

Emerson was thirty-three. He said he wants a younger driver alongside him and I signed politely. To do so, I had to turn down a fantastic contract with Paul Newman. The decision wasn't hard professionally, though I was going to miss that team. I had been negotiating with Marlboro McLaren until five minutes before signing with Emerson. Emerson said he didn't want me racing him in Can-Am; I yielded. After all, it was a step towards victory in F1.

So it seemed at the time. It was the beginning of still more troubled times.

Fitti

Detroit 1984, and there are hot rumours, supported by Emerson's presence, smiling, mutton-chopped, a swarthier Clint Eastwood, in the paddock, that Fittipaldi wants to go racing again. He is shopping about for a drive. Keke spent some unhappy times racing for the Brazilian, whose talents as a driver were not matched by his ability as an organizer.

The talk of Emerson coming back shows that the man hasn't really matured. His last success was practically back in the days of Stirling Moss, though he continued racing long after he'd notched up his championships. A man who's really grown up would know a return isn't on. F1 is a different world today from when Emerson drove well; it had changed by the time he was driving less well.

It was the same story in 1980. Walter Wolf's old team had merged with Fittipaldi. Emerson was supposed to be the number one driver; I was his number two; Peter Warr was to run the team and Emerson's brother Wilson took care of the financial end of things. But even then Emerson hadn't really grown up. He kept fiddling about with the team and interfering with the professionals who were trying to run it in a professional way.

I think Emerson was naive. If I had been in his situation, I wouldn't have dreamed of interfering with Peter Warr. Peter has the ability to organize a team; he has the experience. Emerson could have offered help, yes; but interfere, no. In the end it didn't matter because the team failed. It failed financially. Because someone was daydreaming and the big one was always just about to materialize.

It was really only thanks to Peter that I managed to survive those years with Fittipaldi with my head still screwed on. Peter was supposed to be running a racing team, but he wasn't: he was running a creditor's office from dawn until dusk. He felt a deep responsibility, not only towards the team but also towards all the people it employed. At the time I thought that was a mistake. Peter, like everyone else, should look after himself first. None of the lads who worked there and got their wages more or less regularly understood what Peter was doing or respected him for it. But they got their money, even if it meant Peter himself wasn't paid for months. I didn't get paid on time, but I got paid before Peter because he made sure of it. It took miracles to keep the ship afloat and it should have sunk long before it did.

Emerson was not a competent manager of money, or of much else. Wilson, his brother, was. He's a completely different sort of man. But Wilson was sitting in Brazil and it was Emerson who had day-to-day charge of the team and he fed Wilson a lot of poor information. Wilson is the sort of man who says yes or no, not *mañana*, but he never knew the true situation.

I got on all right with Emerson. Especially at the beginning, when we used to train together at Guarujá, running every day on the beach. But I knew that in the team it was Peter Warr, Harvey Postlethwaite and Peter Mackintosh who had really urged me on Emerson as his number two. They outvoted Emerson, who basically didn't want to know. Maybe it was because I had to be paid; maybe he didn't think I was any good. Everything went well until I started beating him, which was pretty early on in the season. He didn't take to that. Yet at times he could make the most extraordinary gestures. In Montreal I think I qualified sixth and he was sixteenth or something and we were the only two drivers on the grid who didn't have a spare after the massive shunt at the start. He gave me his car and didn't race himself. It was generous, but also by then he had probably decided he was going to quit at the end of the year and just devote himself to running a racing team. I had signed for another two years the night before.

I never knew Emerson in his prime, so I can't tell how good he really was; but you don't win the championship twice without some qualities. He probably was not my sort of driver. He never was, I hear, an attacking, aggressive driver. By the time I was racing alongside him, he was no longer among the very quick. But then we both had less good everything than the rest of the field: less good gear-box parts, less good engines. A team with those financial resources can't run properly; it has to skimp.

We rarely came to open argument, the one exception being in São Paolo, which was the first race I did as his number two. I overtook him in the race and he went off a lap later in front of his home crowd. When he got back to the paddock and talked to the TV, he blamed it all on me. According to him, I was an idiot. Really, I had passed him as I would any other slow car on the circuit; we didn't have anything in the contract that said I wasn't allowed to pass. But the TV was all over me, the press quoted Emerson: 'You put this guy behind a wheel, he undergoes a change of personality, like Clay Regazzoni.' Peter calmed him down, but I honestly expected to be sacked. The meeting in the office the next morning got quite out of hand. Emerson went on and on about me, and then Wilson, who was running the meeting, said calmly, 'I've seen the video, so shut up, Emerson. You're wrong. This thing is over.'

That was the end of it and it was never mentioned again. I respected Wilson a lot for that, because, as the Brazilian papers were to point out, the Fittipaldi family sticks pretty closely together and Emerson, after all, was *their* champion.

I did what I could to influence the team from my number two spot. I drove my heart out. When I wasn't doing that, I was trying to find my way out of the two-year contract because I could see what was coming. There was no future in that team for me personally. I am an egoist; I am interested in my own future. I have to be. No one else is going to look after me, and certainly not the Fittipaldis. I wasn't liked. They didn't believe I could do the job. To be more specific, Emerson didn't like me. Emerson didn't think I could do the job. For the last six months of that last year I was working to get out of the team.

It goes to show how varied is the work you have to do in F1! I call that work, but it was really two problems that required legal solutions. The first was that I wasn't getting paid. I hadn't been paid for ten months. That's a long time. The second was a more subtle problem: how could I create a situation in which I could leave, but make sure I was paid before I left? Neither answer was easy, but it worked out in the end. By an hour. Luckily in my six years of racing I've found a smart lawyer.

I had to leave. Emerson was trying to sell me, but I wasn't at the time the sort of property people were willing to pay money for; and if any buyer did come along and he had to pay Emerson, who was going to pay me? The whole thing was complicated by the fact that Emerson said that he wanted to keep me. Understandable, since I was the only asset the team had left. There were no buyers.

I gambled. I pushed the whole affair in a certain direction. It worked. It got a call in California from Williams asking me to test for the team. By the time, twenty-four hours later, that I went to see Frank in Didcot, I had a letter from my lawyer saying that I was clear of my contract with Emerson. If I had that clearance, I thought I could get the actual drive and not just the test. It was a big gamble. The gamble paid off and I even got my money from the Fittipaldis, probably again because of Wilson.

9

The Fittipaldi Desert

The record of these wasted years, 1980 and 1981, at Fittipaldi speaks for itself. Keke disputed twenty-four Grands Prix for the team – as well as seven non-F1 races – and his best result was at the very start, with a third place in Argentina in 1980 achieved in adverse conditions: stifling heat and a stop in the pits to top up with fuel. Those were Keke's first points in F1. Keke betrayed a surge of optimism:

'I'm very happy and I have high expectations for this season.'

Brazil brought into the open the conflicts latent between Emerson and Keke; Keke finished ninth. The record thereafter is dismal: retirement in Kyalami, eleventh in Long Beach, seventh at Zolder, not qualified at Monaco, retired in Spain and at Brands Hatch, not qualified at Hockenheim, retired in Austria, a fifth place in Imola, then ninth in Montreal. He was far more sanguine than his results allowed, more generous at the time than his later judgement on the team. Again, he wrote his father:

'Half the season was an unhappy time for me; I was driving age-ing cars. The new F8 is a tribute to Harvey Postlethwaite. It is an excellent car, but it's potential has yet to be realized. The team has come through adversity in style, thanks to its esprit de corps. That is all-important, and that is why I have re-signed. My tenth place in the championship, *ex aequo* with Daly, Watson, Jarier and Villeneuve, is highly satisfying for a first complete championship season in F1. Many drivers have made worse beginnings and gone on to do better things.'

At the same time, in 1981, war was breaking out between FISA and the constructors grouped in FOCA: basically over who was to control the sport. Keke was clear about the consequences and the causes:

'The trouble rests on a duality of powers between Bernard Ecclestone of FOCA and Jean-Marie Balestre of FISA. There will be no winner from this war; the sport itself is a sure loser. I am not directly affected as I have a two-year contract with Fittipaldi and I will race where and when I'm told to race by my employer, with or without FISA's blessing. Meanwhile, Skol, our principal sponsor, has dropped out because of a change of ownership and we are still hunting for a new one. A further problem is the search for a new driver. Our choice is between a competent driver and one who comes armed with money.'

Chico Serra, who has become a very close friend, was the eventual choice for 1981, sponsorship was partial and irregular, money was wanting and the F8 from which so much was expected had been designed to run with skirts, which were now banned under the FISA–FOCA compromise. Again, in 1981, after a promising beginning at Kyalami, where Keke was placed fourth, the season declined: fifteenth at Long Beach, ninth in Rio, then three retirements in a row, plus a failure to qualify in Monaco, then a twelfth in Spain. The ending was the most painful of all: two retirements and then three successive failures to qualify. His fourth place at Kyalami failed to count: it was a FOCA-only race and didn't count for the championship.

As for Keke's judgement on Emerson, Fittipaldi's results in his last year of racing were a third in Long Beach and a sixth place in Monaco. In practice he was consistently behind Keke. To his father, Keke expressed the ultimate degradation of racing in such circumstances:

'I've lost all taste for racing. Emerson hands over a cheque and I drive his car, I think, for money. I have the feeling I've become . . . a whore, but even the cheque doesn't make me happy.'

Pride

A curious quality, pride. There was a time when it was considered more of a virtue and less of a vice. Perhaps in the sport pride should be distinguished from conceit. Of which there is a lot. Oddly enough, and contrary to expectations, one gets relatively little conceit from drivers; a lot from team owners, some of it beyond all proportion, as with Enzo Ferrari; a fair amount from engineers, who live in a world all their own; and the most from the hangers-on who have no real part to play in the world of F1. I like to think that drivers have pride. And that, because they live in a precarious world, they are competitive without being conceited. The good ones do not throw their weight around. If anything, they are a fairly reticent lot. When I look about the paddock I see many an ego, often an exuberant, twitching, vibrant, hungry ego, but I do not see prima donnas. That is because driving an F1 car is dirty, hard work and there isn't time for braggards; if a braggard comes into the sport he'll quickly have the corners cut off him. What Keke's remark means is that his pride is objective. He sees himself from the outside; he can place a value on pride.

I'm no more proud of what I do than I would be in any other profession. I'm proud of having found a job that I like and I'm proud that I do it well. But I don't think of it as being better than what someone else does. I make a better living than most, but that doesn't entitle me to look down on other people. There is a difference between being pleased and expressing that pleasure, and being proud and expressing that pride by looking down on others.

I was proud when I won the world championship. Yes. That was a job well done. Only thirty people a year in the whole world do the particular job I do. That's what it's all about, and you can be satisfied if you are one of those thirty.

There are teams which deny you even that. They don't think F1 is special because of the drivers. F1 is special because it's a platform for the most sophisticated techniques of motor sport, because it is extreme, at the far edge of innovation. Drivers are not that important: after all, they don't exist unless they have something to drive around. I don't think the public buys that. It buys one individual racing against another. The public does not follow the constructors' championship; it follows the drivers' world championship.

But for Frank Williams, the constructors' championship is a matter of pride. Ferrari rates it pretty evenly; if anything, Ferrari exalts the drivers a bit. That is odd, when you think about it, for they use their championship for marketing purposes, like Lotus. But nothing more. I don't see where the pride lies in that. I understand that it's better than winning nothing, but I'm always surprised that Frank doesn't see that the drivers' championship is the heart of the matter. I would be proud if I had created a car and found and sustained the driver who won the world championship.

Pride is inner satisfaction. In what you do, you are good, very good or the best. There is no championship quite like the F1 drivers' championship: not in its imponderables, not in its variety, not in the things that can go wrong, nor in the things that can come right; not in the consistency required to become champion; not in the determination, the stamina required. In no other form of sport do you have to race sixteen races in a frail machine, a machine that can betray you at any time, against a number of other people who are so nearly your equals that there's practically no difference between the top six or seven. In no other sport do you race on four continents under every kind of climate, in sun and in rain, on streets and on circuits. Just being a part of that calls for pride.

Sex

Q. Alan Jones said driving a car competitively was in some way connected to sex and power.

A. No.

Q. Don't you feel more powerful in a car? Isn't a car an extension of masculinity?

A. All competition, if you're successful, adds to power. You derive power from competing against others and if you beat them, yes, you feel more powerful. To pass someone during a race is to give yourself a boost of power. I am more interested in the satisfaction of winning than in the power. As for sex, if you look at a driver's harness in the cockpit and realize how the belts squeeze all the blood out of your balls, I wouldn't describe the feeling as at all sexy.

Q. I think he meant not that it was sexy, but that it was like sex.

A. That's a very narrow way of looking at life. At that rate you'd think there was nothing else in life but sex. There are lots of other things in my life besides sex. Sex is sex and racing is racing. They have nothing to do with each other. How could they?

Q. He saw sex as conquest.

A. Then he doesn't get much out of sex.

Q. . . . and that a machine was like a woman you had to seduce.

A. For me it's a war. A war against others and against myself.

Public

I don't mind being touched. I just smile. The public has its advantages. No driver really likes being worshipped. I don't. But I can tolerate it. I get paid for it. I get paid for everything I do. If it makes his day for some Italian fan to shake my hand or have his mate photographed alongside me and I've got the time, I'm not giving that much away.

Drivers' attitudes probably differ. Some of us are shyer than others. Sometimes the public doesn't understand that we have a job to do at a race and they come at the wrong time. Some drivers are better at public relations work than others. But some of the most famous have made it despite having a terrible attitude towards the public, like Lauda or James Hunt.

Niki's money is in his face. Wherever he goes, he's recognized. He doesn't shake that many hands.

Illness

For much of 1983 Keke was ill after a post-championship jaunt with Niki Lauda and John Watson through the less sanitary parts of South America. It was one of the many obligations that fall on drivers: what the sponsors want, they do; that is what they get paid for. Keke's championship year cost him a year of lowered vitality with a serious hepatital infection.

Being ill was a blessing in disguise. It was the first time in years that I had five or six weeks in which I did not think about racing at all. I disappeared to Mauritius and put everything right out of my mind. And that included business, much of which is related to racing.

The first few days I had withdrawal symptoms. I kept hanging about the telephone until I realized the calls from the office were getting fewer and fewer and then that there weren't going to be any at all.

Being ill made me realize the importance of resting, of switching off completely. From now on I shall do it at the end of every season. I hope as a healthy man and not because I'm sick. When I came back from Mauritius, my batteries were loaded; I wasn't fully recovered but the rest had made a world of difference.

I didn't even look foward to 1984. I was 7000 miles away from the team, so what could I do about developing the new car? When they're actually building a new car, my influence is zero anyway; my job is to test it when it's built. Normally Frank Williams will call me regularly and we'll keep in touch on developments. But during those six weeks Frank only called me once: just to say he was alive. He was very good about it.

My time off didn't affect Williams much. It affected my business a lot. I had doctor's orders to cancel everything and I did. I lost a lot of money, but it was worth it. But I suspect Frank was the most worried about my health: he can't use a driver who is half fit. He had just signed a long-term contract with me and whenever he called he would ask, 'How is my investment doing?' He was very happy when he finally got the message from me saying I was completely fit. Whatever their ostensible attitudes towards drivers, teams know that the driver is an important link in the chain they are building for success. They can't do without him.

Sponsors

Some you find; some come to you.

The technique is to spread the net wide. I naturally meet a lot of people from different companies in the course of business or when moving around, or at the circuit. Ortwin does it more systematically. He has a round of people he sees. Also, Ortwin and the PR agency do all the deals. I don't have any time for that sort of thing. The only contact I have with sponsors is when I'm working for them.

Williams Grand Prix Engineering and Rosberg are two quite separate commercial identities. The two only come together when it's a question of timetables.

I admire the Brabham team. There's a good feeling there, and Gordon Murray is a genuine character, a highly interesting man. I threw the idea up in the air a few times, that I should drive for them, but it never came to anything and they never took it seriously either. I could never solve my money problems with them. First, because Bernie Ecclestone is not prepared to give a driver enough money, and second, what is more important, he does not give his drivers the kind of commercial freedom that the agency needs, the freedom to make deals outside the team.

Although ICI also sponsors Team Williams, their public relations pitch is mainly based on the man, not the car. I meet their guests during Grand Prix weekends, between warm-up and the race, and I entertain their customers, go to dinners, show up at trade shows which is invariably the case. I don't mind that sort of thing, so long as it's properly organized. What I hate is to be pushed forward like a puppet and expected to come up with something intelligent to say. If it's well done, you merge with the crowd; you meet some interesting people.

Sometimes, you blow your cool – though not to the point of slugging someone, like Alan Jones did. After all, I get paid to be polite and to smile. But at one sponsor dinner one of the big customers was drunk. I don't remember exactly what I said, but I suspect I was sharp: I shut him up completely.

Williams

Quiet, intense, a recluse, brought up in strict boarding schools far from home, Frank Williams is the odd man out in the raffish gallery of team owners and managers. By now, the old men among this select crew (they number barely a dozen) are reduced to one with the death of Colin Chapman. That one is Enzo Ferrari, with whom Frank has a little more in common than is immediately visible: particularly a huge and easily wounded pride. Neither bluff and extroverted like Tyrrell, nor obsessive and quicksilver as Ecclestone, Frank is dour, smart, tenacious. One thinks relations between the man with the clockwork mentality and the self-centred but more genial Finn might have had their difficulties. In fact, they did not start off well.

Just before I was signed up by Williams, Frank ran about telling everyone he'd just signed the greatest driver. Then the contract was signed. A week later he told one of my sponsors that . . . well, you know, you kind of need a driver but the driver's not very important, he's just there to drive the car round in circles. That's the way the game goes. It's a very commercial world and you say what you have to say at the time you have to say it. Often that means saying what you don't really think because that way you get something else you want. Drivers don't always tell the whole truth to constructors and team managers about what they want and need to get what they want and need; likewise, constructors don't always tell drivers and sponsors the whole truth about what they can afford.

I like to think that Frank thinks better of me than that. We have a very good working relationship most of the time. I respect him and I assume he respects me. Neither of us talks a lot about the respect we have for each other.

I am as close to Frank as I can get, being only a driver. You can't get very close to Frank. In a way we have little in common; we are just in the same line of work. I gave up trying to get close to Frank two years ago. I came to see he didn't want to make friends. Perhaps he has enough. He's a very close man; he probably doesn't need more – more friends, more anything, apart from success – than he's got. Frank would probably say, 'Of course Keke and I are friends.' In his way we are. In my way, we are.

Drivers and team owners and managers are in a very special relationship of dependency. Rosberg is not Rosberg without a car to drive; a Williams is not a Williams without someone to drive it. Finding the exact balance between two egos in search of self-expression can never be easy. Driver or constructor: either can make or break the other. The constructor depends on his driver for far more than racing; he requires from him the technical information on which to base the development of his car. This sort of stuff is not found out in wind tunnels or in books, nor can it be drawn on the backs of envelopes. It comes directly from the driver. But if driver and manager fall out, the driver will wind up the loser. That's when even the proudest driver finds out what a peon he truly is.

Friendship inside or outside a profession are based on the personal tastes and feelings of each person. Everyone thinks differently, which is at it should be. Frank is a deeply competitive man whose life is based on competing twenty-six hours of every day. He is utterly unrelenting. As he said in an interview once, having been at the bottom and worked his way up, he has a very intense fear of falling back. That's the spur that keeps him going. It's walking along the narrow path: very risky, because one slip and you're down. It's the high tension in him that makes him tick. He's got two things in his life: running and racing. Those two things and his family.

I think that is significant. Frank sets great store by human values. In fact, he's raised them to such a high point that it's hard to follow. A very moral man. He puts a high value on his good relations within the sport but he has an odd way of going about building them.

Frank believes he looks after the mechanics and the work force in the factory, that he truly cares about them, rather like an old-fashioned benevolent paternalism. It has led to this joke. Frank goes up to a mechanic and says, 'How are you, Bob? How's everything going?' and Bob answers, 'Well, Frank, my wife died last night.' And Frank says, patting him on the arm, 'Great! Just great! Just keep on doing just what you're doing!'

There's a little malice in all jokes. The fact is, I can analyse Frank but Frank can't analyse himself and I can't analyse myself.

I sometimes wonder whether you can ever be truly intelligent and successful in anything you do, including F1, without studying people and their relationships. In motor sport, relationships mean a great deal; the sport is a network of friendships and acquaintances. Is it possible to accept that there are relationships in the sport which depend solely on use?

I don't think I see human relations quite like that, but in general I think it's true. I suppose relations inside the sport are not like relations outside. They say the same thing of prison! But despite that perhaps slightly unpleasant side, that you may have to use or be used, the contact with so many different people is interesting in itself. When I was on the outside looking in I thought that F1 was interesting because I loved driving racing cars and F1 cars were the best, and because it contained a hell of a lot of interesting people. Early in my career people played a bigger role than now.

I don't really ask to have a personal relationship with anyone in F1 any more. Not with Frank or with anyone else. I don't know whether I'd see Frank if I weren't in motor racing. Would I find him an interesting man? I'd probably go and see him when he's racing, because that's what we have in common.

As the situation stands, I'm in racing to win races. If Frank is down and the team is down, naturally relationships are going to be among the early victims. However, I like to think I have the best possible team boss: one who is every bit as competitive as I am. And if the relationship didn't pay off on the private side, it was paying off on the professional side. So I put things in their proper order. Competition comes first for both of us. Everything else comes after.

You ask if you can be super-smart and successful without some deeper human dimension. I have to answer no. Thus Frank is 95 per cent the best possible boss. The extra 5 per cent isn't there.

But the 95 per cent is better than what most team managers have to offer. You can't be perfect. And maybe I'm lacking that 5 per cent myself. I enjoy looking into others but, like Frank, I don't enjoy looking into myself. Why not? Maybe I'm afraid of finding something I don't like. Maybe that's the way with Frank, too. I'm pleased with my life as it is; let's assume he is too.

It would be equally true to say I analyse my personal life quite a bit. Maybe Frank does too. But that's not the territory on which we meet.

Go back to Fred Opert, who not only gave me my real professional start but also taught me a lot. Paul Newman was another. He was a man I really related to: he was straight, he was laid back, he was smart and he was a friend. I like him more than I know him, but the point is that I also liked the people around Paul. We were a family, and one of the things I've grown to dislike about F1 is that there are no longer any families, no longer any feelings. Now it's all business and who gets whom. I've had more than a few intimate insights into that aspect of it.

Think of my relationship with Jacques Laffite: since we've been racing together there must have been times when he felt they weren't crazy about him on the team. For no good reason whatsoever, because I can't imagine a better team-mate. Perhaps his results weren't what the team were hoping for, but in terms of the relationship Jacques and I formed one of the best teams you can imagine. And I'm sure that over a long championship season human relations inside a team contribute greatly to success. Good human relations. We have plenty of the other kind, too.

And I'd have thought, too, that having lived through the really fraught situation between Carlos Reutemann and Alan Jones, where those relations deteriorated seriously and damaged the team, Williams would have appreciated better than most teams how important communication and human relations are.

That's just not the way it is. It's not that way at Williams and it's not that way in most teams. For instance, look what happened to Patrick Tambay and to John Watson. They were loyal, they suffered through the bad years at Ferrari and McLaren, and suddenly they are dropped. Loyalty? Feeling?

All this was gathering inside me like a knot, and then at the end of 1982, just as I was winning the championship, I found out that I was being offered to another team. As a trade-in.

After that, I ask myself, where is loyalty? The answer is: there isn't any in F1.

I keep a good relationship with Frank, I enjoy it and would have liked it to have been deeper. But after that piece of disloyalty, that's not going to happen. I knew all along that he was a hard man to get close to, I knew he was obsessive, neurotic in some ways, but it's my nature to like people, to like working with them. But when I found out about that, I said to myself: I can't figure out people who behave like that, I won't ever know what makes them tick, they're too unlike me. And I stopped trying to read Frank's mind.

No one needs to like someone else to be able to work with him, God knows. I re-signed with Frank, and the wind started to blow in the opposite direction. I thought I'd been hired by Williams because they thought I was capable of driving racing cars fast, and developing race cars to the point where they could be driven fast. I did my best. I got the results. I beat Jacques square. Then, if under even those circumstances there are people in the team who doubt your ability and want to get rid of you – I don't say it was Frank, or just Frank – you've very little hope of making your situation stronger.

I've thought it all out since then. I've asked myself often enough why they tried to get rid of me. Was it really because I wasn't good enough? Was it because of my personality? All I know is, I certainly wasn't going to ask.

Sometimes drivers get traded for commercial reasons. That wasn't the case with Williams. I know to what team I was offered and for what driver. It wouldn't do my reputation any good to put on record the name of the team or the driver who was supposed to come to Williams. Let's just say it was a driver who has yet to pick up any results.

Sometimes drivers have to move because they ask for too much money, like John Watson. That wasn't the case with me. I was still cheap. I'm not cheap now, but I was at that time.

Wattie is a very good case. As a friend, I feel sorry for what happened to him, but as a professional colleague, I think he dug his own grave. Mind you, he only did what I would like to do: he said to himself, 'I belong to this team, I've given them good results, this is where I want to drive.'

He got a good warning at the end of 1982. He should have known exactly where he stood at McLaren. What Wattie didn't learn, what I have learned, is that in F1 the main question seems too often to be who stuffs whom first. That isn't the attitude I brought into the sport. It's an attitude I've had to learn the hard way, right through my heels.

It took people a year and a half to tell me that Team Williams had tried to trade me. The friend who told me had been afraid of hurting my feelings. They, at least, knew I still had some feelings that could be hurt. They tried to spare me, but, in fact, when I did find out, I got another sharp lesson. It's the sort of lesson which, once it lodges in your brain, nothing's ever going to drive out again.

It doesn't change my personal attitude towards anyone in the team; it just teaches me another lesson. And from Wattie I learned, or had reinforced, something I'd realized early on in the game: that you never stop looking elsewhere. He should have been hunting hard for another drive in July. I start hunting in May. I don't care about the niceties, whether Ferrari says, 'We contacted Keke' or 'Keke contacted us.' The truth is I contacted them. And not just them, but many other teams.

Why should I teach other drivers what to do? The truth of the matter is that, unless you have a long-term contract, you should keep looking around. That's what I do because it's logical. Unfortunately for them, too many drivers don't look around until it's too late and all the doors are shutting in their faces.

Being a professional means looking after your own future. No one else is going to do it for you.

10

Victory

Keke's championship season, which was also his first season with a major team in F1, started off in fraught conditions in Kyalami in January 1982. The cause was a quarrel between the drivers, grouped in the Grand Prix Drivers Association (GPDA), and FISA. Superficially, the quarrel was over minor matters; in reality, it concerned track safety and a widespread feeling among the drivers that they were being treated as the least important element in F1. Thanks to the intransigence of all parties — the GPDA led at the time by Niki Lauda and Didier Pironi, FOCA by the unyielding Bernard Ecclestone and FISA by the equally stubborn Jean-Marie Balestre — the drivers decided to go on strike.

Those of us who were there can well remember the scene that early morning on the Kyalami track. A bus was parked some hundred yards down from the paddock and as the drivers arrived, singly, they were stopped and led into the bus. When their number was complete, the bus left. It suffered a brief halt at the bottom gate of the circuit as team-manager John McDonald tried to block its departure, but Jacques Laffite, among others, got out and pushed McDonald's car off the road. The first and only official drivers' strike was on. It lasted the rest of that day and through the night: a night in which the drivers lived in a meeting room of a downtown hotel, slept on the floor, held endless emotional meetings and, in between, were entertained by the clowning of Bruno Giacomelli and the piano playing of Elio de Angelis.

None of it was Keke's scene. He joined the strike and went to the hotel out of loyalty to his fellow-drivers, not because he approved of a strike. He was not a member of the GPDA and has always refused to become one. He was not, and is not, a joiner by nature.

I thought it was ridiculous; if it had depended on me alone, I would have gone right through the so-called picket line, got into my car and raced. After years and years of work I had finally made it to the top: to a first-class team in F1. Now I was being asked to take part in a strike that I knew had not the slightest chance of succeeding. I was really conned into the strike without knowing what had been planned; I was given phoney explanations. Furthermore, I knew exactly how Frank Williams felt about it: just like Bernie Ecclestone, who fired Nelson Piquet and Riccardo Patrese the moment they said they were going on strike. I thought Frank would do the same; I would have if I had been in his shoes. Also, strikes are no way for intelligent people to achieve their aims.

I was totally conned and therefore didn't have much choice, though by nature I'm entirely against strikes, boycotts or anything else of the kind. Motor racing is not a sport for that sort of thing; we are all too egoistical. There is nothing more rowdy, ill-behaved and self-defeating than a GPDA meeting. Everybody states his own point of view, no one listens to anyone else, and at the end of the day nothing has happened but a lot of time has been wasted.

I've had no reason to change my mind since then. On the contrary. Pironi and I fell out over the strike and how it was handled. In my opinion, much of the strike garbage was his doing; it was like a high point in his life. Much more important, I never felt it was the drivers themselves who were acting, but that there was some power behind Pironi and Lauda. Much of the material we were given had obviously been prepared outside the motor racing family. My suspicion—which I cannot prove since I was not asked to join, probably because my views on joining anything are well known—is that there was a move afoot to set up a sort of superstar agency to negotiate with the constructors, circuits, sponsors, etc.: a sort of Mark McCormack for motor racing. The idea of a group contract goes against everything I believe. I never got a straight answer when I asked who or what was behind what we were doing, but I didn't need it.

As for Niki, I think he fell into a trap. Or maybe it wasn't such a bad idea for him at the time. After all, he has the name and the fame that could indeed be marketed by such an organization.

1981 had been a complete failure for me in F1 and I was not interested in doing anything that could jeopardize my career.

Keke

In the event, Kyalami 1982 was a hot race in every sense. The temperature was in the nineties and Keke was seventh on the grid: the top position for a normally aspirated car. Arnoux was on pole for Renault. He stayed in the lead for thirteen laps and was then overtaken by Prost, who eventually pulled into the pits with a puncture. Keke made a good start, was third until overtaken by Pironi and Lauda, and eventually finished fifth. Prost won.

It was more than I had done the whole previous season. I was delighted and so was Frank. But Kyalami was also the first place where water tanks built into the wings began to play their part. The tanks were filled before the race, emptied during the race and then refilled to make up the weight at the end. There was no other way to ride on even remotely equal terms with the turbo cars with their greater power.

The Argentine Grand Prix was next on the calendar, but financial difficulties forced a cancellation. The striking drivers were all fined, but Keke remained a happy man. At last he was in a top team and had proved that with a decent car he could perform and finish in the points.

Brazil was next and Keke qualified third on the grid, three places ahead of his team-mate Carlos Reutemann, who was ostensibly the number one of the team. The heat was again tremendous. Keke, as original as ever, did an extra warm-up lap by passing through the pit lane. Villeneuve took the lead in the race, followed by Arnoux, with Keke fifth. After Villeneuve went off trying to get by Piquet, the race became a straight fight between local hero Piquet and Keke. Nelson won; Keke was second, his highest placing in F1. A place that FISA was to deny him.

At the end of the race, exhausted, but not as exhausted as poor Nelson, who actually passed out and whom I had practically to hold up on the podium, I found out that Ferrari and Renault were protesting our one-two. Their protest was rejected by the stewards of the meeting, but they appealed first to the Brazilian Federation and then to FISA in Paris. Frank and I had a sneaking suspicion what would happen there. We got the news after Long Beach that FISA had upheld the Renault–Ferrari protest. 'Maybe FISA wants a French champion' was what I said before Frank made me shut up.

What gets me is that we'd raced in Kyalami under exactly the same conditions. And not just Williams, but a lot of teams. All of us were interpreting the rules as they stood at the time. Other cars with water tanks were doing better times than we were. And the Williams team does not cheat. But there is always snooping along the pit lane and rivalry between the foreigners and the English teams that leads to endless protests and politicking.

No one denied that we added water. So did a lot of other teams. Only Piquet and I were disqualified. How can that be just? Alan Jones had won at Las Vegas with water tanks, and two weeks after Brazil Lauda and Watson were to win Long Beach with water tanks. Could FISA prove that we had been running light? Of course not. It was just a presumption. As I see it, every race is a separate event. If there is a gap in the rules and you want to plug that gap, then go ahead; but do not punish people who acted honestly in accordance with the rules in operation at the time.

I consider myself a sportsman. Nelson and I had driven a fine race in gruelling conditions; we had finished one-two after giving the spectators full value for their money. I was leading the championship, having given it my all. Now politics was going to take that all away from me. That was the first time I got stuffed by FISA and the reason was ridiculous. If Piquet and Rosberg, why not the others? Maybe the others were not important at that stage in the championship.

The next race on the calendar was Long Beach. The FISA appeal weighed on all the team, as well as the unexpected departure of its official number one driver, Carlos Reutemann, who suddenly decided to retire. Reutemann had been due to test the new FW08 in Europe, which would have allowed Keke some time to prepare for the California street-circuit race; instead Keke had to go and test at Dijon. Fortunately, the new car was a success, though Keke had hoped to persuade the Williams engineer Patrick Head to fit carbon-fibre brakes. His appointment as official number one driver, however, boosted Keke's morale.

It was all a little ambiguous at the beginning of the season, and though the relative positions of drivers really doesn't carry that much weight in a first-class team, I wasn't really at ease. But having

Mario Andretti for a one-off drive at Long Beach was an excellent idea, and being now confirmed as the team's number one driver did wonders for me. Also, we finally had a spare car. But the track had been altered and slowed down, and a lot of new surface had been poured, which always causes problems.

I was on pole on Friday practice, but on Saturday I just couldn't get the car to hand and the best I could do was eighth.

Andrea de Cesaris was on pole and Keke made a good start, but a sudden move by Pironi – into a gap that wasn't there – cost him several places. De Cesaris went off and Lauda took over the lead.

The race was made memorable for me by another, and probably the last, real tussle with Gilles Villeneuve. Andrea had gone off early on, Niki was leading and Gilles and I settled down to do battle. He was much quicker than I was on the straights and I was better in the corners. His rear wing was a big one and didn't seem to be properly fixed; when Gilles finally tried to out-brake me on the outside on a corner where such a manoeuvre was impossible, he went off. After that it was easy and I finished second behind Lauda. Though the turbos were giving up one by one and I had my own doubts as to whether Niki could stand the pace, he was unbeatable. My tyres weren't that good but at least I'd enjoyed the battle with Gilles immensely.

It was when we got back to England that I heard FISA had upheld the Renault–Ferrari protest against Nelson and myself, simultaneously depriving me of my lead in the championship. I was extremely bitter about it. That was part of the bad blood that led to the Imola boycott. The sport was at war again and I was disgusted.

At Imola, the San Marino Grand Prix took place with only the so-called 'legalist' teams participating – all turbos – and a few of the lesser non-FOCA teams then loyal to FISA, a total of fourteen cars in all. Ken Tyrrell was the only FOCA participant. The race itself was made remarkable by a brilliant duel between Didier Pironi and Villeneuve. Pironi carried the day with a superb overtaking manoeuvre in the closing stages. Villeneuve – rather as was to be the case with Arnoux and Prost – was furious at the 'disloyalty' of his team-mate and even refused to congratulate him on the podium.

I watched the race on television at Paul Ricard where we were testing and felt furious and frustrated. If a race is going on, we should be there. I thought I'd have a real chance at the championship and we weren't even racing. In my opinion, it was not a positive decision.

Zolder in Belgium came next and the new Williams FW08 was ready. It was an immediate success.

We'd been to Zolder for testing and I knew right away the car was going to be outstandingly good. We beat the Renault turbos out of sight and only Piquet's Brabham was faster on the straights. Naturally the 'legalists' had to do something about that and the result was that Zolder was the first race in which it became illegal to add water or oil at the end of the race.

I welcomed clarification of the rules, but they still created almost impossible conditions. Today we have a man who travels the entire season setting up and testing the scales which are used to weigh the cars, but at that time each circuit had its own scales. We would weigh the car at the factory in Didcot and it would be within the regulations; then we would go to a circuit and the weight would be completely different. There was no way to test the scales' accuracy. It didn't matter what your car actually weighed; what mattered was what those scales said. And what would happen if your car turned out to be 200 grammes under-weight? It would make no difference whatever to your performance, but legally you'd be under the weight. It made all sorts of difficulties for us; it became a headache to consider the weight of usage and wear in brake pads, oil, tyres and so on, to take everything into account. Niki actually got disqualified at the end of the race for being under weight. If he had stopped at the end of the race he would have been within the weight, but he probably used just enough fuel crawling back to the pits after the race to put him underweight.

On Friday morning I was fastest in practice, but by the after-noon I had slipped down the grid to eighth. Between Friday and

Saturday the team worked hard to find the defect and on Saturday morning I was again fastest. I was finally third, behind Prost and Arnoux, during official practice. Prost was a tenth of a second faster. Frustrating. The turbo only required a turn-up of the boost for qualifying and they were unbeatable.

Shortly before the end of practice we heard Gilles had had a terrible crash. I was numb. I didn't want to talk to anyone. It didn't really hit me then; I suppose I was kept intact by the fact that I had a job to do.

On race day I had a problem in the morning warm-up and my engine blew. It affected my confidence. Maybe Gilles in the back of my mind, maybe I was worried about the new engine. I don't know, I just wasn't at my best. But once the race got going all that left me. Arnoux took off first and I got in just behind him. Prost had not made a particularly good start and was third, I decided that Proot wouldn't get by me, but I was still nervous; all I knew was that I had to stick to Arnoux. After four laps, I got by him. That was the first time I'd actually led an F1 race. I went a little wide at one point and, miraculously, the car actually handled better after that.

I was delighted to have blown off the Renaults – so much for their changing the rules! – and everything was going well except that I could see from the pits that Watson was catching up with me. He seemed to have exceptional grip on his tyres. Mine started to go halfway through the race and were just about finished twenty-five laps from the end, at which point Wattie was a little over a second a lap faster than I was.

On the second-to-last lap, I made a mistake, but Wattie would have taken me anyway. We were both coming up to lap Marc Surer. I knew I had to pass him before the next chicane and put him between Wattie and myself. That was my one chance to finish ahead of Wattie. I went for it, locked my wornout rear tyres and ran wide: it was a piece of cake for Wattie to get by me. What I tried probably wasn't possible, but it was the only thing that might have worked. If I had got by Surer on the next corner, it would have taken Wattie a few seconds to get by. If he had had to catch up with me during the last lap, I could have held him.

At the time I criticized Surer, which was wrong. I had a go at catching him because he was there. He wasn't in my way, but he was the man who was either going to allow me to win my first race or wasn't. He was the last little bit of the package. Now that I have had time to analyse it, I understand he did nothing wrong; but at the time I had to decide everything in a split second. He was my rabbit; I was just about to shoot him. Instead, it all went wrong.

Frank, too, was sore. He thought I should have won and he didn't hide his feelings. He wasn't the only one. A lot of people were saying I'd made a mistake, and they were right. Yes, I'd made a mistake. I'd made a mistake because I was going too fast for the condition of the car. I was losing all the rubber on the rear tyre and having a lot of trouble keeping the car on the road. The disappointment of losing a possible first win was bad enough.

I had moved back into third place in the championship with those six points for second place, but in fact the picture was far from rosy. I was still upset by those anonymous people sitting in Paris taking away my six points in Brazil, in effect saying Rosberg didn't deserve those points. The politicians had deprived me of a chance to race at Imola and now I'd blown another possible three points. All right, the points were gone, but it still rankled. It put a lot of pressure on me at the time. I wouldn't have described the atmosphere in the team as optimistic about the championship after Belgium. I felt that Frank was also under a lot of pressure from somewhere; it transmitted itself all the way down the team.

It was one of several low points that year, and if a driver reaches that sort of low, then there's trouble. No one can work properly if he's low. It's easy to say you should be able to put such problems out of your head and just get on with the job; it isn't always that easy to do. You can have a low for one race, but when you hit a whole low period – Brazil points gone, Imola gone, a possible win gone – then it takes a real effort of will. Only you yourself can pull yourself out of the shit.

Coming into Monaco, Prost led the world championship, followed by Watson. Keke was third. After the various setbacks, Keke was fully aware of the importance of the race: a very special race in any case.

The mystique of Monaco is probably due as much to good marketing as to anything else. To my mind, it's head and shoulders above any other Grand Prix in Europe: because of its unique setting, because it's the best street circuit in the world, not just 90 degrees around the block, because of its variety, its features, its challenge.

It's not a race in the strict sense of the word. No street race is. I would have Monaco as the only street race in the calendar. That doesn't mean I like everything about it. It's a hard place to move around in, it's a hard place to work in. Also the track is tricky and in several places dangerous. I like neither the uphill, where if two cars bang wheels no one know where you might end up, nor the chicane, which is too fast. I never feel I am in control there. Likewise, I don't like the start, which is crowded, narrow and short before the first corner.

But in 1982 I had other problems as well. Most important of all, I had to try to get on pole, because that's the only place to be in Monaco, given that opportunities to pass are few. Then I had to drive carefully, because Monaco is also a very punishing circuit. In 1983, when I won the race, it was actually a bit dull. I had a huge lead and everything was happening behind me. I remember Arnoux getting pushed 100 yards into the pits and going back out on the circuit afterwards: naturally no one would ever black-flag a Ferrari at Monaco! Only Rosberg in Brazil! But that's F1.

We had made a number of modifications to the car for Monaco 1982, and the team wasn't particularly up. I just concentrated on getting my own adrenalin going, frankly. I try to pay attention to the feelings of others in a positive way: come on, cheer up, let's get the job done. It's easy to be happy when you're on top. At the time we weren't. When things are not going right, it seems an insoluble mystery.

Keke was third in the first day's practice. Friday belonged to his sponsors. Saturday he tried again, but the result was disappointing. Instead of his much coveted pole position, he fell back to the third row.

There were a couple of drivers out on the circuit who refused to look in their rear-view mirrors. They blocked the road. In Monaco, of all places, what can you do? The warm-up on Sunday was just as bad; I was slow and the track was so bumpy down by the swimming pool that my head was bouncing around like a ball. I knew my problems were two: to make a good start and nurse my car so that I could at least finish.

I was eighth into the first corner. Both Alboreto and de Cesaris overtook me, but in front of me Arnoux spun and Giacomelli retired. That put me sixth and I was chasing Alboreto. He is a gentleman and let me past. With Andrea, I had more trouble. I always do. His attitude is that if someone's on his tail trying to get by, he should prevent it by any means. Twice I got right alongside him; twice I couldn't get by. At that point we were fighting for fourth place and we fought each other for forty long laps, during which the car was so hard to handle that I actually took the skin off my hands just holding onto the wheel.

I knew I was faster than Andrea and it was in one of my attempts to get by him that I broke my suspension. It was another mistake. I knew it was the one place I really had to watch and still I hit the kerb. That's what sticks in my mind from Monaco 1982: by misjudging an inch and a half I blew it and hit the kerb. Andrea's engine was sick and I'd been alongside him twice. I knew where I might be able to get by him, but I'd been following him for so long that I had got into his rhythm, and when his engine faltered I wasn't able to adjust quickly enough.

But I still think I can get a magical result at Monaco every year. It's my sort of track. An inch and a half is all it takes at Monaco to defeat you. It was my first retirement at Williams and it hurt: but not as much as my hands, which looked like two pieces of steak.

The next race was the first Detroit Grand Prix. In the opinion of most who lived through its travails, it was hardly an unqualified success. Keke himself was particularly disturbed by the slowness and inadequacy of the preparations.

Everybody showed up as usual, but the track wasn't ready. No one knew what it was like, no one had tested; all we could do was walk around the track and see where there were likely to be shunts. There were plenty of possible places. It was a bit dispiriting to sit for a day and a half in the coffee shop while they were getting their act together; all you could do was sit around, sleep, shop and get loot in the Renaissance Center. After a while I began to wonder not when things were going to start but whether they'd start at all. To make matters even better, it was pissing down with rain and I felt as though I was in a prison camp. I didn't get a breath of fresh air for two days. We couldn't organize anything else because the Detroit people kept saying the track would be ready in ten minutes or half an hour.

You could say I've obliterated that race from my mind. I don't like the circuit and never have. It's tight, boring and bumpy.

Derek Daly had taken the place of Reutemann and that was, for Keke, a considerable change from the superficially phlegmatic, but ever anxious, obsessive Argentine.

We got along well together, but I can't help thinking that Derek was someone who tried too hard. He couldn't relax at all and the fact that I was regularly quicker than he really got under his skin. That affected his performance. He was one of those utterly fearless drivers like Gilles, but it seemed he couldn't learn what you need to learn to be successful in F1 – a little patience and a little discipline. It was as though he had this huge bubble in his brain and it was always about to burst. He is a much better driver than his performance in 1982 showed, but he didn't last in F1 because of his temperament. He just could not cope with the pressures he put on himself. He had a terrible accident in 1984, and I think that was as inevitable as it was with Gilles.

At the time he may already have been having marital problems. It's not the sort of thing drivers talk about, so I can't really judge the effect it had on him, but he was edgy. When I saw him again in 1983 he was a changed man, enjoying himself much more, much more relaxed.

The only thing I can really remember about the Detroit race is when I passed Prost. We passed and repassed each other and I finally got past him. There were two starts, the second after Patrese hit the wall and the organizers brought a tow-truck onto the track. I knew then that I had a chance because the new grid was set by the positions we were in when the race was stopped and I was then second alongside Prost. His tyres looked worn to me, while mine were still in good shape. Then I got by him with something under an inch to spare between my car and the wall. I was in the lead and the closest threat came from Pironi. Then the Williams pit signalled that Wattie, who had started seventeenth, was only 12.9 seconds behind. I thought, Damn! Is he going to do a repeat of Belgium on me? It took him just three laps to catch up and pass me! His tyres seemed to be magical. I went after him as hard as I could, but my gearbox gave way: third and fourth gears were useless half the time. Cheever and Pironi got by me and it's a miracle I lasted through to the end. But my feeling at the time was that luck was simply not smiling on me: not just in Brazil and Imola, but now in Belgium, where I could have won, in Monaco, where I made a mistake, and in Detroit, where I had led again and could do no better than finish fourth. Even worse, the Ligier cars had been found to be illegally wide. Disqualified? No, the team was only fined.

The three points were some consolation, but not much. Wattie had won two races on the trot, but I was still third in the championship. At the beginning of the season, you calculate that's it going to take 50 points or so to win. I had 23 and we were practically halfway. When you're building on a basis of two points here and three there, it looks a hell of a long way away. If you have two or three nine-point victories under your belt, it's a piece of cake, or used to be, before Prost proved it wasn't enough. In that sense, Wattie looked a lot better placed than I was. I had to take Wattie seriously. Drivers come in two basically different types: the attackers and aggressors, and the sitters and waiters. Watson was a chameleon. No one does the sort of over-taking he did at Detroit that year and gets away with it. But when he does a thing like that it is all the more extraordinary because it is out of character. Normally he is patient. You don't expect it from him. And he was the one guy who looked as though he could really take the championship away from me. Combine that with the knowledge that it isn't every year that you're going to be in a position to make a real attack on the championship. Of course I was worried after Detroit.

Even when we got to Las Vegas at the end of the season, my rational mind was telling me: Don't underestimate Watson and don't forget your engine could blow on you. There is a part of me that is deeply pessimistic. Wattie never did become world champion; it escaped him that year. Who knows why? Perhaps his temperament wasn't right. But that's not what I was thinking halfway through the season. John has a completely different mentality from me, but that doesn't mean he wasn't every bit as good a driver. You could say – and people have – that the championship goes to people who are harder and tougher than Wattie, that he was too nice. But after Detroit I was hardly in a position to rest on that fact and say, 'Hey, this man isn't thinking right, he's never going to win, he can't touch me, I'm the guy who's supposed to be champion.' No, you know you're going to have to work hard for it, race after race.

Finally, weariness was setting in. I was doing all the testing. I had asked to do it and Frank gave it to me. That was part of the concentration on the main thing, winning the championship. I'm lucky that the team gave me that chance.

Montreal didn't promise to be any easier for us. It's a difficult circuit against turbos and my attitude going there was: What chance have I got on that circuit? All season, if there was a chance on paper that I might get a result, then I had fought. But there were some circuits where I knew I would be handicapped, and Montreal was one of those. I also had a few memories of 1980 when an accident between Piquet and Jones had sent me into the wall and turned my car into a crumpled mess.

Still, by the time practice started I had recovered some equilibrium; I was going well and was determined to forget the disappointments of the past few months and go for it. Friday practice went fine; I led both sessions. Then on Saturday it started to rain. My engine blew. When I went out in the spare car it was all but undrivable. Somehow it had not been set up right. It bounced all over the place; it wouldn't steer properly through the esses. The best I could do was seventh on the grid and, despite all the work done on the car on Saturday night, I was only ninth during the warm-up on Sunday morning.

Pironi was on pole, but he stalled at the start and I only just managed to get past him. I was luckier than some of the drivers further back on the grid. Poor Riccardo Paletti didn't see

142

Pironi's car, hit him in the rear and his car caught fire. He died instantly.

It was two hours before a new start could take place. Again, there was trouble, with Mansell and Giacomelli shunting. Arnoux was then in the lead and I was sixth. That didn't last long, either. Piquet took the lead, I dropped back and seventeen laps from the end my gearbox went. As several of the leaders dropped out with fuel starvation, I could have been in the points. It was another disappointment to add to all those I had suffered during the season. I had dropped back to fifth in the championship and neither I nor anyone else thought I had much of a chance left. For three races now, I had failed to score a single point.

That was the low point of the season: a mistake at Monaco, a poorly performing car at Detroit, failing to finish in Montreal, and problems piling up. It's not the sort of situation calculated to make you cheerful. But it's a funny game, F1, and when you're on the inside you know that what you have to do is simply pick up the pieces and work all the harder. You have to tell yourself that the game isn't over.

I wasn't the only one discouraged. Frank and Patrick Head and Frank Dernie and the whole team were down. It was at that point that Frank tried to trade me off to another team for the following year. I suppose it's reasonable to think that inside the team management they were saying, 'Well, what can you expect with two unknown drivers?' That sort of attitude was bound to permeate the whole team: the mechanics worked as hard as ever, but I could tell that they were down too. The pressure was on all of us. The Williams team had been all-conquering in 1981 with Alan; now with me and Derek it seemed to be falling apart. Frank was edgy; Patrick was edgy. Teams go through low points and that was ours.

Good teams know how to ride the disappointment. Between Montreal and Zandvoort the Williams team worked hard to improve their car and repair the psychological damage inflicted by their recent defeats. Keke went testing in Zandvoort itself, at Paul Ricard and at Brands Hatch. By now Didier Pironi was his chief rival for the championship, though not the only one, and in early testing at Zandvoort he was a full two seconds faster than the Williams. Patrick Tambay had joined Ferrari in place of the deceased

Villeneuve and the race was scheduled for Saturday in order not to conflict with Wimbledon. On Thursday Keke was seventh in practice; Friday it rained. Arnoux was on pole.

I had some trouble seeing the starter's signal and by the time I got the message a lot of cars had got past me. Still, I somehow got into queue among the first ten. After about ten laps I managed to get past Giacomelli and Lauda, but saw that one of my tyres was losing pressure. I knew I had to pull out all the stops anyway, so I took off after Tambay and got past him. Up front were Pironi – the Ferraris were superbly reliable – and Piquet. The two Renaults had once again dropped out and Niki was well behind me and no real worry.

The last ten laps I really drove on the absolute limit. Forget nursing the car, the tyres, the engine; I just drove as fast as I could. On the last lap I had Piquet in sight, then I was right up on him; on the final straight I was right on his tail. The car, the tyres, the engine had nothing more to give. But third place was, at last, a positive result. And three points put me back in the running a little. But Pironi had added another nine points to his total and, to the world at large, he looked the best bet for the championship.

Zandvoort is the race where we finally pulled ourselves up out of the slump. It was important for that. Watson hadn't scored and it was now a three-way battle for the title. Or so everyone was saying. To tell the truth, I wasn't really concentrating on the championship at all. Maybe it was too sweet to dare to think about. I was just trying to drive as well as I could. The championship was too tight for anyone to build any solid hopes on, and coming up from the bottom, from bad times, the whole team had to pick itself up off the floor before even thinking beyond any one particular race. The first time I seriously considered the championship could be within my grasp – forgetting the beginning of the season until FISA robbed me of my points – was in Austria, and it wasn't until Dijon that I actually set that as my goal. That is the curve: a high at the beginning, a huge drop in the middle and then a slow rebuilding.

In a way it's a good lesson to learn: not to be discouraged when things go wrong and to realize that, as long as it's mathematically possible, the championship is still within your grasp, especially when, as in 1982, there were so many contenders within striking distance. I think Prost must have faced the same problem in both 1983 and 1984 and I felt for him. When the season begins, the championship looks a long way away; in the middle of the season, a driver may falter. If he loses interest then, when things that were going right suddenly start going wrong, he is giving it away.

But Brands Hatch was going to be my race. I knew it in my bones. I could stay at home and concentrate on the race; the circuit was favourable to the Williams and unfavourable to the turbos; my only real worry was the McLarens with Lauda and Watson. On Friday I had a minor brush with Arnoux which put him off, but I was still able to set pole position: I broke my own record by a full second. Victory seemed in my grasp. But on Saturday afternoon – a very hot Saturday afternoon by English standards – the car was not performing well. I had thought I could do even better than on Friday, but in fact I made no progress at all. However, I still stayed on pole. Sunday warm-up was even worse: there were five cars quicker than I was and I came back to the pits in an unhappy frame of mind. The aerodynamics of the car were not good, the engine didn't sound right and the whole car was vibrating, which was bound to affect the tyres.

But Brands remained one of the circuits best suited to my style of driving and I kept my hopes fairly high. It's a track where I feel I'm fast and my first pole position had filled me with confidence.

I knew the problems of starting at Brands. I had to place my car pointing slightly downhill into the wall to avoid a slide. I had it all figured out. But not the fact that the engine wouldn't start. The fuel pressure was vapour-blocked. We made several tries before the engine finally turned over, and I took off to catch up with the rest of the grid, which I only did at Clearways. A disappointment, but no disaster. I said to myself, 'You're going to win from the back and that will look even better!' I was so quick in the car at Brands that I knew I couldn't be beaten. Seventy laps is a lot of laps.

However there was another problem. Goodyear had come up

with a new tyre and we hadn't really tested it properly. With the full tanks, we'd had a serious understeering problem: maybe, we hadn't done enough testing with full tanks. As soon as the race started I knew the problem was a real one. I had reported it, but the team hadn't managed to solve it. When the light goes green, it is too late to worry about that because there's nothing you can do any more. All you can do is go for it.

After ten or fifteen laps I was sixth, but I knew my front tyres were going to be a problem. I had a lot of understeer, and then the front tyres let go. It wasn't as if the problem was a new one. People outside F1 don't understand just how finely tuned an F1 car has to be. If you are understeering the tyres are going to heat that much more: where a 10-degree turn would do under normal circumstances, if you're understeering it takes a 15-degree turn to produce the same effect. You are simply rubbing your front tyres off and that is going to slow you down.

When I came into the pits I could see the team was in despair. There's nothing worse for a driver. He's sitting there in the car, fuming and waiting for something to be done. He thinks he can still save the race: so what if he has to change tyres and so what if he knows the understeering will destroy the second set like the first? But when he sees the team trying to do a quick change and not being able to get it right because everyone's in a panic, his world collapses around him. I expect the people in the pits to keep their professional faces on, at least to stay calm and pretend that everything is still all right. But there were Patrick Head and Frank Dernie with faces ten feet long. I looked at Frank Williams and he was just as gloomy. Not only was their world falling about their ears; mine was too, and it was my race.

Then, when I got going again, the engine had a misfire and finally stopped. I gave up. 'Now we're equal,' I said when I got out of the car. 'I blew Monaco and you've blown this race for me.' I really let them have it. I was furious because I felt betrayed. Here was the one race of the season in which we were absolute favourites and we'd blown it.

Worse yet, we were heading into a group of ultra-fast circuits that definitely favoured the turbos. Ricard was next, and if I was to achieve a good result there it would have to be due to a miracle.

146

Keke was not wrong. During practice at Ricard, the turbos were a full five seconds faster than the Cosworth-engined cars; what was worse for his hopes, the turbo-engined cars were also making considerable progress on the corners. The best Keke could do on the Friday was sixth. Lauda was fifth and Prost provisionally on pole.

On Saturday afternoon Niki braked right in front of me on my quick lap and I had to slow down; the result was that both of us fell back on the grid, Niki to ninth and me to tenth place. There were words between us because I was sure Niki's braking had been deliberate: he'd made a gesture as he passed me which wasn't in keeping with the way a man of his stature ought to behave. We sorted it out on Sunday and Niki admitted he had been wrong. That's the great thing about today's Niki: you can talk to him about anything. Still, that was my worst grid position of the year and matters did not improve after the start when I went off the circuit briefly on the first lap and dropped back to twelfth. Fortunately, there were a number of retirements ahead of me – Patrese, then Daly, then Lauda, then Piquet. That made me fifth. Alas, my tyres were also going and Alboreto was catching up fast, but I was able to hold him off after a long struggle.

That was the race which Arnoux led and in which Prost lay second, which was not the order Renault wanted to see. They signalled for Arnoux to let Prost by, but Arnoux paid no attention. Afterwards, Prost made a bitter attack on his team-mate. I was in trouble throughout the race: no wing, no handling, worn tyres. I finished all in all fifth, behind Tambay, but the situation was not promising. Hockenheim was next, another circuit where I couldn't hope for much against the turbos and I was fifth in the championship.

Hockenheim is far from being my favourite track. It's an unimaginative circuit and the chicanes are an artificial obstacle which I detest. My attitude was a little negative. There were still 45 possible points to be won. At Hockenheim I didn't expect to be much better than seventh on the grid and I had acknowledged to myself that Pironi was most likely to be world champion. He had a solid lead, an excellent and reliable car, and he was driving particularly well. I knew that at Hockenheim I certainly had no chance of finishing ahead of him.

It was hot on Friday and in morning practice the turbos dominated as expected. The one surprising thing was that Niki was well up the grid and some six seconds faster than I was. I thought he was up to some trick and said so at the time. In official practice that afternoon Niki spun off the track and injured his hand, but he was, as at Ricard, a place ahead of me. He was ninth and I was tenth. Pironi was on pole ahead of Prost.

I had hoped to claw back a few seconds the following day, but when I woke up it was pouring. Only a few drivers went out testing in the morning, but Pironi turned in an excellent time. He didn't need to improve it, but he went out again and, running behind Prost and Daly in a cloud of spray, saw Daly braking but not Prost. The result was the third serious accident of the year and the end of Pironi's driving career – and of his hopes for the championship.

The track didn't dry out for the afternoon session, no one improved his time and the grid lined up with Prost alone on the front row.

During warm-up my engine had hiccoughed at high revs and I decided to go out in the spare. The team managed to get it ready at the very last minute, but I hadn't gone out in it and I hardly knew how it was set up.

It wasn't a pleasant race. Piquet was put out by Salazar and tried to hit him, and Patrick Tambay led the race, with Arnoux behind him. I more or less inherited third place after Prost and Watson dropped out. That at least kept my chances alive and, with Pironi out, I suppose they were better than I thought. But my thoughts didn't extend that far. Once again my car had been unsatisfactory, I'd had to wrestle with it to bring it in for a place on the podium and, to cap it all, when I got back to England my house had been emptied of everything I really cared for.

Just a week later the championship moved to Austria. Niki Lauda had made some foolish statements to the press to the effect that it would be a disaster if Keke won the world championship. Keke was justifiably irritated, but the needle is part of F1 and Niki is a man who feels a psychological need to be on top, not just in driving but in every way. It should be remembered that Niki was in his first season back in F1 after his retirement, that he was not in a prominent position in the championship, where his team-mate Watson was well ahead of him, that he was the most highly paid (and famous) driver in the sport, and that he was suffering from a certain amount of neglect. The two men respect each other, but for temperamental reasons they were not close friends: in part because of Keke's refusal to participate in the GPDA and in part because Niki considered Keke selfish, self-concerned, brash and a relative parvenue who was climbing too fast in F1 without having acquired the manners and poise of a possible champion. However, relations have improved greatly since.

None the less, of all Keke's races, the one that probably remains most engraved in the public mind, is the race he lost to Elio de Angelis at the Österreichring during that championship year of 1982. It was a race in which the two cars finished barely a length apart after a fiercely fought race and in which both drivers displayed to their best what the public expects of F1: close combat, skill, courage and sportsmanship.

Where one is placed in a race or in the championship is important, of course, but you have to take into account all the factors which settle the matter one way or another. To have finished fifth in the championship in 1983 made me neither disappointed nor elated. No one who had had to struggle through that season with a normally aspirated engine did any better and fifth is not bad for a non-turbo. It would have given me immense pleasure to have been first, but that wasn't ever likely to happen.

I can't say that I take immense pleasure, either, in finishing second in a race – unless second is all I need for the championship. The one exception was in Austria where I had an immense battle with Elio. Boy, would I love to have won that race! But I was aiming for the championship, so second wasn't bad. Besides, I like the young man and it was his first win. I was pleased for him.

I was in considerable pain from my foot and I lost God knows how many seconds during the race because Jacques Laffite blocked me when I was lapping him. Apart from that, no excuses.

The race came down to the final corner, a long right-hand curve down the hill, with Keke right behind Elio for one last attempt to move past the black and gold Lotus.

The truth is, I wasn't brave enough to get past Elio on the last corner. I could have done it. That is, if it hadn't been for the championship being at stake and for the fact that it is such a quick corner, I could have gone straight over the kerb on the inside. There is plenty of room and no obstruction. But at the top of the hill I hesitated too long, trying to figure out which side I should go on on the way down. At the end of the day, I think I was right. What good would it have been if we'd had a shunt?

Five years ago I would have gone on the inside: over the kerb and through the grass. But, looking back on it, it was difficult to predict what Elio would have done if I had tried it on on the inside. Once inside, I would have had no chance to go back. Also, five years ago I might have underestimated de Angelis. By the time of that race I no longer underestimated him: whichever way I'd tried to go, he would have sought to block me.

The only chance left to me was to out-accelerate him coming out of that corner. It didn't work, but I wasn't far off. A hundred more yards and I would have made it. I tried, but the hundred yards weren't there. Even if I'd known in advance it wasn't going to work, I'd have still tried it. As I say, five years ago I'd have been a braver man. No, probably more stupid. Everyone matures; one's thinking changes. Life changes, and I think more than I used to. It's instinct. It's not something you teach yourself. Elio thought out that race just as I did. He won it as a mature driver wins a race: by making no mistakes.

I remember getting out of the car and saying, 'One more lap, please!' But the six points I had won suddenly put me in the lead in the championship and it was at that point I began to take it seriously as a possibility. Once you're ahead, after all, it is up to others to take it away from you. I had just re-signed with Frank – whatever his doubts had been during the dark mid-season, he was now full of encouragement – and the world was looking better. The race had been one of those that gripped public attention. The only oddity was that here was Rosberg leading the championship and he hadn't yet won a Grand Prix. There were sections of the press that wouldn't forgive me for that, but I didn't give a damn. The championship is the championship whether you win it with four Grand Prix victories or by consistency and a lot of lesser places.

None the less, Dijon, which was next, was the sort of circuit where a driver's talents dominate. I knew I had a chance there, and Jackie Stewart came up to me and said that if I shaved my moustache I'd have an even better chance. Actually, by this time, Jackie had changed his mind about me; he was man enough to admit he'd been wrong. With some drivers, that's when they get superstitious, when suddenly the title is within their grasp. It's like tempting fate. The photographers crowd around you, everyone wants an interview. The burden shifts to you. You lead the race; now it's up to you to prove that you deserve it.

The turbos beat me in practice. On Friday I was beaten by both the Renaults and the Brabhams and also by Niki and by Andrea de Cesaris. The problem again – despite all our testing – was understeering. We decided to put on a bigger front wing and during Sunday warm-up the car was greatly improved.

I made a very good start, overtook a lot of people on the outside at the first corner and came within an inch of tangling wheels with Niki at the esses. Niki didn't see me, but I managed, just, to avoid an accident. Prost was leading, with Arnoux second, and I was soon close up to René, but when I came up to lap Andrea de Cesaris, my whole progress was suddenly halted.

To the best of my memory, there is only one occasion in my driving life when I've come close to losing control over myself during a race. Dijon was that time. There I was running third and catching up on the leader at about 1.5 seconds a lap, which is pretty quick. Then I came up against Andrea. He was very quick on the straights, very slow in the corners. I lost eleven seconds behind him. He just would not let me by.

I lost control. I was on the verge of becoming dangerous. If it had been possible I would have got out of the car in the middle of the straight and hit him as hard as I could straight in the face, climbed back in the car and gone on. It all went through my mind. If I had a long stick in my hands I would have banged him on the head.

Would I have shoved him off deliberately? I don't know. I was very close to doing so. We were both going down the straight at 170 m.p.h. and I banged him with my front wheel on his sideboards. I couldn't get any closer. I could get my front wheels between his wheels but my old Cosworth couldn't do any better than that. I knew I would be home on the next curve, but he out-braked me time and time again on the outside.

Andrea was a lap behind and I was desperate for a good result and some championship points. Still, I wasn't going to risk trying to out-brake him in those circumstances. I finally did it because Andrea made a mistake. I had my front wheel in front of his front wheel, my car somehow managed to veer all the way to the left and Andrea had only two choices: to go off or lose it. He chose to go off. Nothing happened, but he was all four wheels off and bloody well deserved it too.

Finally, I got Arnoux and then I caught up with and overtook Prost some three laps from the end. I was a bit surprised: he went wide and the door was open. There were three or four corners left before the long straight to put enough distance between him and me so that he couldn't catch up. I had my right front tyre blistered from the early stages of the race, but it worked out in the end. I won the race and for the first time I really set my sights on the world championship. That's when it began to seem real.

It was also my first Grand Prix victory, but what really mattered was the championship.

From Dijon, Keke went to Monza to test for the next race. He was beginning to suffer the indignities visited on prospective champions. He couldn't rest, he couldn't find any privacy and his business interests, with the championship a real possibility, began to consume him. Testing itself was taxing. The heat in Monza was extreme, and at Brands Hatch, where he tested possible set-ups for the final race at Las Vegas, he went off into the catch fencing from pure fatigue. But rest was difficult to obtain, and although Keke arrived as late as possible at Monza he was immediately besieged. In theory, he could win the race at Monza; in fact, the circuit did not favour the Williams and Prost was the clear favourite. Though weary and irritable, Keke maintained enough sangfroid to describe his position with great precision. He thought he would finish in the points, but low down; on the grid, he ought to be, by his calculations, about seventh, behind the turbos.

At Monza I knew I would be struggling. The opposition in terms of the championship was Wattie, but Prost was still very much in the hunt. Monza is never easy. The fanatical crowd makes it a very intense place; the circuit is very fast, the weather is hot and there always seems to be that little extra bit of pressure.

I ran the early part of the race in eighth place without trying too hard. All I needed was one point and so I was running a strictly tactical race. Giacomelli overtook me on the straight and I heard a bang which I thought was a tyre; I had to slow down and several cars went by and I returned to the pits, telling the mechanics to change the tyre. But it was the rear wing that had broken. The pit stop took two minutes and I had fallen back to fifteenth. Arnoux was in the lead and Prost was third, but after he had changed tyres he spun off: that was the end of his championship chances. Watson managed to finish fourth and keep himself in contention. The race produced nothing but disappointment for me, but at least the title was now between two men. There was still hope.

I decided the most important thing for me was to relax. I stayed at home from Sunday to Friday and went to California early, with the intention of relaxing in California until just before the race. I needed to recover physical and mental equilibrium. I was beginning to suffer from the effects of the long season and also from the prospect of the amount of work that lay ahead of me if I was going to win the championship.

I arrived at the track in Las Vegas at the very last possible moment. Once again it was very, very hot. I could barely breathe in the cockpit of the car and the temperature on the track was something like 130 degrees. On the first day of practice I was fifth, and afterwards I had to face some idiotic questions from American television. They kept asking me if my only motive for racing was money. They started to get under my skin and I was short with them. The pressure was building up, though I wasn't really conscious of it. During Saturday practice I fell back to sixth. I was a little bit disappointed.

I knew the situation perfectly well. The task ahead of me was to finish the race in a certain position without even thinking about what Watson might be doing. It seemed entirely possible to me, but you never know; you never stop thinking about what can go wrong.

The Renaults led at the start and I was soon in sixth place. There I had a battle with Mario Andretti, but Mario's suspension broke and I got by him safely. I was then fifth and the stakes were clear: if I had to retire and Wattie won, I was going to be pipped at the post. The pressure was on Wattie, but he was again in brilliant form: he had made a bad start, but he was third. Prost and Alboreto led, but Prost was in trouble and Watson got past him. My fifth place was all I needed, but if I retired and Alboreto retired, Watson would be champion. It was my fifty-second Grand Prix and everything I'd been working for since the start of my career was at stake.

When it was all over, Alboreto won, Wattie came second and I was champion, I felt an enormous sense of relief. Whatever anyone said about my being lucky or not deserving the championship, the fact was that I was champion. I didn't care how I'd won it; I knew I had more points than anyone else.

The press had joined Niki in saying I wouldn't be a brilliant champion. To me it made no difference: brilliant or useless, I was the champion. I agree that a champion has certain obligations; to some extent he belongs to the public. But I saw no reason why I should suddenly become a glamorous champion and throw parties and celebrate and carry on as though I was different from the Rosberg who had worked hard and fought against all disappointments to become champion. I was going to be myself.

That day was Mansour Ojjeh's thirtieth birthday and he went to San Francisco to celebrate. It was a great party with great people. There was a specially made cake – a Finn had won the championship and there was a great shark's fin sticking up out of it. We went out to a pub, we had a lot of fun, we rolled around in an open 1936 Rolls-Royce, singing, dancing, drinking, eating hamburgers. Maybe people like the Ojjehs come from a different planet than the rest of us when it comes to money, but they are an example of very rich people who are also completely natural. They have big hearts and they treat you as friends should be treated.

But I was too tired – too overwhelmed physically and mentally – to enjoy the party properly. I was miserable and in no mood for a celebration. I had no intention of getting drunk and forgetting that particular day, so I left early. I think that is probably characteristic of winning the championship. There is a sudden deflation as you let go of your control and realize how exhausted you are. It's a few days later that you wake up and find the world still has something to offer.

I had worked hard all year, doing all the testing, driving the whole season often under adverse conditions; I'd been through despair and hope and mental stress. When it was over, it was like a balloon. You let the air out and all there is left is a pile of rubber. That's how I felt.

11

1983

The year after a championship year always begins in uncertainty: can the momentum of one year be carried forward into the next? In the case of Keke's 1982 championship, the question was doubly pertinent, for Williams had taken the decision, unwillingly, to continue racing on their old Cosworth engines until they could find a suitable turbo engine. They were thus at a disadvantage against the big turbo brigade. These, in their turn, had made substantial progress in solving their own problems: the cars reacted more quickly to the throttle, were less wasteful, were somewhat lighter and had proved – already in 1982 – that they were no longer merely quick on the straights, but also as competitive as the normally aspirated cars in corners and thus could no longer be disregarded on the tighter circuits.

For Keke it was to be a difficult year. Although there was a natural momentum remaining from being champion, the other teams had not stood still. All of them, as the championship began in South America, had improved cars ready or in the wings. None of this was unknown to Keke: he was not sanguine as the year began and, as it progressed, he became increasingly depressed with the underperformance of the old Williams. There was nothing he could do about it. The new Honda-powered Williams would not be ready until 1984. Meanwhile, he struggled on as best he could, knowing that he could not be truly competitive, that repeating his championship win was beyond his powers.

Once again, the beginning of the season was blighted by a FISA decision which disqualified him after a brilliant race. He had been on pole and fought magnificently, despite a fire during refuelling, to finish second behind Piquet in Brazil for the second year in succession. In Long Beach, full of aggression and determined to show that he was a worthy champion, he drove a spectacular race, spinning early on and resuming the race brilliantly, only to be put out later by Jarier after first brushing wheels with Tambay.

Towards the middle of the season, a series of decent, though unspec-
tacular – apart from Monaco – results put him among the championship
leaders. Though the handwriting was on the wall, Keke's results – fifth in
France, fourth in Imola, the victory at Monaco, another fifth in Belgium,
a second place in Detroit and a fourth in Canada – kept him fourth, the
table then reading: Prost, 28; Piquet and Tambay, 27; and Keke, 25.
Thereafter, it was steadily downhill as the car became more and more dif-
ficult to handle and increasingly uncompetitive against the turbos. Only
in South Africa, at the tail end of the season, did he score one more fifth
place with the new Honda turbo to bring his total for the year to 27
points, which gave him fifth place overall.

His dissatisfaction was obvious, but mitigated by the thought that the
following year must give him another crack at the title. It was also, as he
recounts, the beginning of deep trouble at Williams. The cracks had
begun to appear after two successive championships. By the end of the
year, despite all the hopes placed in 1984, they could no longer be papered
over.

The Team

It has been very difficult for a team that's been up on top for four
or five years to find itself suddenly – or maybe not so suddenly,
but slowly and steadily – in the shit.

Teams are no different than drivers, in that they too feel the
frustrations of the sport. And one of the worst frustrations for a
team is to be on top and then start the great slide downhill. Often
it's not entirely easy to explain, which makes it worse. You think
you're doing the same things, you're applying yourself as much
as ever, but none the less the slippage is there. Almost all teams
go through a period of this sort. It's even possible for me to feel
sorry for Renault, who have the frustration that, despite all the
money they've poured into the sport, the good drivers they've
had, the talent and the effort, they've got absolutely nowhere.
Ferrari has had its bad years, so has Lotus, so has Brabham. It's
something you learn to live with.

Sometimes it's not merely that you're bad, but that other
people have suddenly got very good. McLaren's bad years were
long; suddenly it's all come right for them. But any member of
that team is still likely to be asking himself, 'What is it that we're

doing right that we weren't doing right before?' or 'What are the other teams getting wrong that they're so bad?' The idea is not to get bitter but to block out the frustration and concentrate on the future. But it doesn't take a genius to realize there's bound to be sand in the wheels when things are going wrong.

Zandvoort in 1983 is a good example. It was the absolute bottom of the season for Williams and for me. I was twenty-third on the grid. Great!

Still, I made a fantastic start. At the end of the first lap I was already thirteenth or something. I was doing a great job and really enjoying myself. I wasn't sitting there in the car cursing, knowing that in ten laps or so I'd be in the shit. It's my job to know what's coming, to take it into account. So I know the tyres are going to go. And if I don't know that, then I've done my testing badly, because I *ought* to know.

But I'm not cursing. I'm having a good time. I hadn't expected the car to work so well. I'm enjoying the feeling of doing my job very well. I've taken risks, I haven't touched wheels with a soul, I haven't endangered my chance of finishing the race and it's all going much better than anyone has a right to expect from twenty-third place on the grid.

So, after ten laps, what happens? As expected, everything falls apart, the tyres, everything.

Comes the end of the race, with the car and me limping home. It's into the pits, back to the motor-home. They're still there – Frank and Patrick and the rest – but they're packing their briefcases; they're already on their way.

I think that is the worst sort of collapse – to run away when faced with frustration. I wanted to talk, the usual briefing never came. That became very typical. You sit on your anger by not discussing what went wrong. They would say it's not very productive to analyse a car that you know is not good enough and is getting worse; not when you can look ahead to next season and a car that's going to be a whole lot better. (Ha!) I think there's always something to be learned, even from a disaster. No matter how big. We're too busy building something new, they say. The new Turbo. The New Great Future. You begin to wonder if it's wise to think so much about the future that you're not even willing to learn from a present mistake that you've paid for. 'Hey!' I wanted to say, 'We've paid a hell of a lot of money to take part in the Dutch Grand Prix and maybe you should try to get something out of it, even if it isn't glory or prize money.'

Nothing. Let's get out of here.

They could have reacted the way I did. The first ten laps were just as they should be: what did we do right and why did it go wrong?

But teams can teach you cynicism, too. Five years earlier I would have been very upset, because I would have expected the team to say, 'Fantastic! You did a great job at the start. We knew the tyres would go, but you did a great job.' Now, I didn't feel anything at all except an edge of disappointment. And perhaps a premonition that things weren't going well in the team.

The entire second half of 1983 was like that. The cars were very bad. They were underpowered; they were pigs to drive. The first half had been terrific, starting with pole position in Brazil – the very last pole position the Cosworth engine ever had or ever will have. A salutary shock to the rest of the world and one which I thoroughly enjoyed. Still, even as I chalked it up I knew the second half of the season would be bad. I didn't know it would be as bad as it was.

Should I have hung my head at the end of the season? I don't think so. I believe I did a good job. Even if the car was uncompetitive, I was still giving the team 100 per cent. That's what I was paid for and that's what I delivered. I have a clear conscience and some satisfaction: at least I'd done my job well.

When things go bad and there are that many competitive personalities, and competing personalities, in a team, you can expect trouble. In 1983 Williams was a happy, if troubled, team. They just blocked it all out and thought about tomorrow. The signs were there. The car was underpowered. We all used that fact to protect ourselves from being too conscious of our failure.

It wasn't a group decision to start blaming the car rather than ourselves for what went wrong. Every individual made that decision for himself. There are always strong people and weaker people in every team; the strong ones tend to drag the weaker ones after them. Our different personalities should blend together, the more they have going for them, the better the results.

Personally, like most drivers, I work better in a happy team. Perhaps the word 'happy' is a bit extreme. Shall we say a 'united' team?

Unfortunately, leading the kind of life I lead, I don't have enough time to do the sort of pulling together I probably ought to have done. There is a lot the driver can do. Whether the team admits it or not, the driver is very much the heart of a team. Some teams accept this; others don't. Ferrari is at one extreme: there the driver is perhaps too much the hero around which everything else revolves. At Williams it is the other way: the driver gets shoved down into his place. Don't raise your head too high, you're just a small part of the team: that's the Williams attitude.

I don't mind that. I can live with that. I don't need someone to boost my ego. Yet I understand how central the driver is to the team. He's the most visible part, the central cog in the machine and, finally, the man who has to go out and get the results. At Williams there are egos just as big as mine at the management level, so a driver can't have much effect. But at the mechanical level, and as a symbol to other employees lower down the chain, the driver can do a great deal. He can help bring it together; he can help create that unity of effort. Mainly by making clear to everyone that he feels part of the team and he is not walking two hundred feet in the air above them. The smart driver keeps his super-star attitudes out of the team he's working with.

That means recognizing that each of us has things which he does better than others do. There are drivers who are good at pulling things together, and those who are not. There are also those who've never given a thought to doing so. Their attitude is that they do the job they're paid for and that's that. That attitude might still net you 95 per cent results, but, if you enjoy your job and work together, that last little 5 per cent can make all the difference. At least it can maximize all the possibilities.

Despair

In the middle of 1984 Keke discoursed again on the situation within the Williams team. What he says applies as much to the previous year as to the one he was now soldiering through with increasing despair. Despair is the right word, for when a man has been champion and knows that he has it within him to be champion again, it is galling to find himself tied to a team that is no longer competitive. Even more galling, perhaps, to realize that the series of mistakes, misjudgements and personal quarrels which upset the team in this two-year period of racing misery were not of his making.

Much hope had been pinned on the new Honda engine. The Japanese constructor, with characteristic Japanese thoroughness, was investing large sums in development. A huge staff laboured on the engine. Honda engineers appeared at the circuit to perfect it. But the mistakes had been made early on: Patrick Head's decision to continue with an aluminium chassis when most of the other major teams had shifted to carbon fibre was just one of a number of wrong decisions that began to affect morale on the circuit. As partners in Williams Engineering, Head and Frank Williams were at loggerheads and their dissention filtered down to the team. It was a case of two oversized egos at war. Keke, who has quite an ego of his own, only just managed to keep his cool. By Detroit, where both Williams qualified at the wrong end of the grid, on a day in which his team-mate Jacques Laffite (who was suffering as much as he, but has a happier, more easy-go-lucky nature) for the first time qualified ahead of Keke, he was in the worst low of his career.

The reason Jacques was ahead of me is that he went faster. Or shall I say that I went more slowly? There is no deep mystery behind it. There were no technical problems. The car had a horrible understeer and Jacques is better with understeer than I am. If I had been third and he on pole, I might indeed have been angry, but as we were nineteenth and twenty-first it didn't amount to a hill of beans.

I wouldn't call this a high point in anyone's life. Things were bad before; we knew we were on a down slope since the middle of 1983 but we didn't know that it was going to be so steep. The whole year had begun badly. We discovered a problem testing in South Africa, namely understeer. 'Emergency' solutions were applied. Seven months later and we were still understeering.

In this sort of situation the natural tendency is to look for a scapegoat. I don't know who was responsible for our comedown in the world. I'd been hired to drive cars and to give information on how the cars behaved. It may be that someone was a bit ignorant about the way I described the car. It reached the point where it was noised about the team that I couldn't really command the English language. That is, I wasn't capable of describing complicated matters about the cars. As I'd had no difficulty in 1982 when we were champions, I suppose I must have become an ignorant Finn since then.

I'm not an engineer or a technical man, so I can't pinpoint responsibility and say that Patrick Head was wrong or right not to change to carbon fibre for the chassis. If Patrick says he can make as rigid a chassis out of aluminium, I will believe him. I know there are always bad moments in development, I know it takes time to develop a turbo engine and relate it to the proper chassis, and I also know, since I've worked with him for years, that Patrick Head is a first-class engineer.

Nor did I have any rows with the team – beyond the kinds of arguments that always take place because of tension when things aren't going well. *I* didn't have any rows, though others might have. I maintained a good relationship with the team, I had no personal problems with any of them. But a driver is a very impatient animal and my patience had begun running out some time ago. I was shit tired of going downhill.

I was helpless. There had been plenty of time, there hadn't been enough progress. I go and test the car at Brands, for instance. After which I tell the team that if all they can do is change a spring ratio by 200 lb they're wasting their time. That doesn't mean to say I didn't think they weren't doing their best; I'm sure they were. But if that was all they were going to do, it wasn't worth bothering. I couldn't put any pressure on Frank. As soon as I tried, he slipped out of my hands; if I persisted, there was an explosion.

All competitive people – and Frank is deeply competitive – feel the pressure. They didn't need any extra from me. I dropped that. I was like a fish in lukewarm water. It wasn't helping my career, but on that subject let's say I was hardened enough to weather it without taking too much notice. What could I do? I'd tested the car for six months and it'd become worse. Either they had to think I was useless at testing, or they'd get around to improving the car. I'd have been a happier man whichever conclusion they came to. I didn't like feeling dead.

Of course, everyone was suffering alongside me. What was one of the best-disciplined teams in the business was going through a bad time. Organization always suffers under pressure. The whole thing became a desperate effort to salvage something out of a miserable season.

12

1984 Bottoming out

If two years after a championship year you are still suffering – from out-rageous fortune, disappointment, pain, loss, inefficiency, confusion, aggravation and a host of other complaints, all of them adding up to a con-spicuous lack of success – then it's natural to complain. In this the driver is no different from any other human being. He weighs his chances when he joins the profession. But as a profession F1 differs from most in one thing: no matter how good you are at it, if your car doesn't have the goods it's like try-ing to win the Derby on a milk-horse. It can't be done.

But drivers also live by eternal optimism. Races come and go. The race that ends in disaster or failure is but one race; there is always the next race coming up. Season follows season; if one season has been poor, surely the next must be better?

After all the bitter disappointments of 1983, Keke's mood between seasons was one of great optimism. The Williams was finally joining the turbo brigade. Honda was an engine maker of almost fanatical discipline. It had the means, the will and the marketing incentive to prove itself against Porsche, Renault, Ferrari, Alfa Romeo, BMW: the big boys. In addition, it was Japanese. That is, it had a presumed technological edge and a wealth of experience in the gadgetry that goes into all F1 turbos.

That 1984's season didn't turn into a triumph was cause enough for bitterness and rancour. In fact, the year brought rather too much of that.

It happens to F1 teams; they go off the boil. In 1984 Williams, which had been uncompetitive in 1983 because it lacked a turbo engine, came near to sliding right off the edge. The pressures are great. There come times when the sheer arrogance of winning brings about an attitude that defeats the whole enterprise. Constant experiment is succeeded by a certainty that whatever you are doing is right, because you are doing it. And when the people who run a team are made up of fairly rigid stuff, are inflexible, stubborn, ten-acious (the very qualities that brought the team to the top), in adversity these qualities militate against compromise and against recovery. In a sense, a team that has been successful and then falls on bad days – and it has happened to every major team in F1, to Lotus, to Ferrari, to Brabham, to Tyrrell – has literally to hit bottom before it can regroup itself. Then, if the resources, human and financial, are sufficient, it can hope to revive. If not, it will go the way many have gone in F1: into oblivion.

It was not the same bottom as Keke experienced when driving for Fittipaldi. This time he knew what the top was; he'd been on top; he was at the top of his profession and to be anywhere else was infinitely galling. Especially when he could say, with more than a little justice, that the failure was not of his own making.

Watching him throughout the year I could see the spiritual barometer fall: from optimism after testing in South Africa at the beginning of the year, to determination after Brazil – knowing that second place there had been a fortuitous result – to slow disillusionment, to perplexity, to fear, to anxiety, to anger and finally to a deeply cynical acceptance of the fact that 1984 was going to be like 1983, only worse. It was another postponement of the realization of his ambitions.

It can have been no better at Team Williams, and Keke's acceptance of that, and of their common task, is a sign of his real coming of age in the world's most competitive, and unforgiving, sport. Drivers' biographies are supposed to trail clouds of glory after them. Sometimes the glory lies in learning to live with adversity. That at least is a truer version of the driver's life.

The exact record of this decline and eventual, hoped for, resurrection in 1985 is charted in Keke's account of a hard year.

Brazil began the troubles because the result flattered the truth. The car was very difficult to drive; it was like a rodeo horse. I was lucky. I held the bull by the horns and managed to finish second after qualifying ninth. That gave the team the wrong impression. The track was bumpy and I couldn't get the car to work properly. I didn't yet know why. It could have been any number of things – so much was new. I told the team the car was just about the worst car I'd ever driven; but what I said probably wasn't given sufficient weight because of the result.

We went to South Africa where we had tested the car during the winter. I was second on the grid after a battle with Nelson Piquet to take pole; I had it the first day, he won it on the second.

I got a good start and led the race for a while, but it was clear to me that the car was not competitive: a great big motorway queue was building up behind me. I had a fun battle with Derek Warwick. He was quicker on the tricky bits of the circuit, but I managed to hold him off on the straights. He just couldn't get by. Shortly after the fuel stop, the drive shaft failed. It lost its lubrication and ran itself dry. It wasn't just bad luck. It was our own fault. There are very few things in F1 you can blame directly on bad luck. Most of the time someone has to bear the responsibility.

On balance, however, the South African race didn't leave us feeling helpless; it just misled us because the car ran well on the straights. Fortunately, F1 drivers are a well-behaved lot; they queue up nicely behind. Still, by then I knew the car had a serious understeering problem. But, I said to myself, understeering can be dialled out of any car. Unfortunately, it didn't turn out that way.

So we came into the first European race at Zolder with mixed feelings. I was reasonably optimistic. Zolder has always been a good track for me; it has the kind of corners I like, third- and fourth-gear corners on which you can make a lot of time. I qualified third. But when the light went green, I couldn't get the car off the line. It was stuttering and not firing properly, and stalled, as it was to do twice again in 1984. I therefore started at the back of the grid. I thoroughly enjoyed the race, however. I was very competitive, having a lot of fun passing people. My only complaint during the race was that the car was – still – understeering and the tyres went off. But everyone was in some sort of trouble and, though I ran out of fuel with half a lap to go, I still finished fourth. I felt I had read the gauge right; Team Williams thought I'd made a mistake. Perhaps I misinterpreted it. Racing drivers have to be drawn maps and charts; I felt we hadn't discussed the matter in sufficient detail. After the race, each went his own way. It wasn't a happy situation and it left a certain amount of bitterness.

It was the only Ferrari win all season and the McLarens weren't strong at all. When you think how they dominated the rest of the season, it makes you wonder what happened after Zolder to make that sort of change.

Just a week later, we went to Imola, where I qualified third. Again, with Prost on pole and Lauda behind me, the engine stalled. I was getting the right attention for the wrong reason. If you're near the front of the grid and your car stalls you're in deep trouble. I was very lucky not to get hit. It happened three times during the season; it was just luck I didn't get hit once. It's not a particularly nice situation to have to sit there and think, 'Oh no, here we go again!'

Niki had said, 'For Christ's sake, this time get off the line,' and I had answered, 'If I do get off the line, you won't see me again.' Which shows there was as yet no despair in my heart. And no sense of how strong the McLarens were going to be. At the time I still thought of myself as the hot shot of the season. F1 dis-illusions you pretty fast. After a couple of laps an electrical failure put me out. With all the problems connected with developing a new engine, you're mentally prepared for things like that to happen, but it's still frustrating. Usually it's just some tiny thing that goes wrong.

Two weeks later we were in Dijon, but in between Belgium and France we had been testing. In Dijon the engine seemed to be going fairly well. We had the same power as the rest of the field; we were at a bit of a disadvantage because of low revs; our con-sumption was not as good as we would have liked, but it wasn't diabolical. The understeer was still there, despite all the adjust-ments. There was a lot of talk in the team about huge changes being made, but the fact was we were not getting anywhere with our main problem.

At Dijon the understeering reached a new low. I qualified sixth and we went three abreast into the first corner. I nearly had a big one with Niki on the fast esses shortly afterwards. I was a bit too hungry. It was I who backed out. I finished sixth in a dull race, running around without being able to do much about it. For some reason we still felt we had a good season coming. We had reliability and the engine was OK; all we had to do was refine the fuel problem and get the chassis right. If we didn't have those problems we'd be fast. That's what everyone says. Solve this and that and you'll be all right.

Monaco was not a good prospect for us. It was going to be a very difficult race because of the bumps combined with our engine's characteristics. Tenth place was lower than I hoped to qualify and is not a cheerful place to be on that circuit. It was also, of course, the wettest race I can remember. It's one my manager Ortwin Podlech will never forget either. He was out lining up sponsors and he got soaked. Team Williams had a new employee to look after sponsors and, when Ortwin came back to the motor home looking like a drowned dog, the new man said, 'What's happened to you?' He was nice and dry.

I agreed with the decision to stop the race. I finished fifth behind Arnoux, coming up close then dropping off from time to time; but there were never more than 200 yards between us. Even that close I couldn't see the track, which meant that whole sections of the track must have been flooded. I didn't feel too confident about either the harbour chicane or the uphill part, so I was quite happy to have it over. It wasn't the sporting Rosberg talking. The sporting Rosberg would have said, 'The longer the race, the better my chances. The hotshoes will go on banging each other, so percentages are in my favour.' The self-protecting mind took over. It said, 'Time to stop.'

Funnily enough, Frank wanted it restarted. He kept me hanging around and insisting on a restart. But I was glad it had stopped without a mess. It was good to have Jackie Ickx in charge of the race. At the morning briefing everyone was delighted that, for once, we had a race director who knew what he was doing. I felt sorry for the flak he got afterwards. He stopped the race at the right time and that's what counts.

After Monaco, we faced back-to-back races in Montreal and Detroit. Montreal is bumpy and fast, with tight chicanes, fast bumpy esses and a hairpin; one is bad for the suspension, another for the chassis, a third for the engine. Either I had no power or full power and in both cases I was in trouble. I qualified fifteenth, had an unmemorable race and Jacques and I both stopped on lap 33, which was the first double retirement of the year.

By this time I had begun to bitch to John Green and John Westwood, my long-time mechanics. They are a fantastic pair and they themselves were in despair. When things go wrong, you lean more and more on people inside the team. From your own you know you can get some moral support, and you're not that eager to face the outside world. Charlie Crichton Stuart had left the team and I missed his laughter; Peter Collins became the person I leaned on most and he took up the slack left by Charlie.

By the next week, in Detroit, Keke had reached a sort of nadir. I interviewed him sitting on the pit wall in Motor City and even I was shocked by his attitude, as was Frank Williams. Like many people in F1, Frank is used to a fairly docile press. It is a small world and everyone has to go on living with everyone else. A bad press, even if what is said is perfectly true, has an adverse effect on sponsors who are far more sensitive to what is said about their team than the team itself. Keke admits that he was at a particularly low point.

I was very depressed in Detroit. I don't really know all the reasons why. Things were no better and no worse than they had been; I was simply resigned to not being competitive in 1984. It was one of the few really poisonous interviews I have ever given. It consisted of facts not camouflaged in the least. I felt that while you can fool some of the people for some of the time, when things get so bad that an innocent schoolgirl can see what's wrong, then it is best to be honest with yourself and tell the truth. That should boost everyone's ambitions to get things right again. I did not intend to be destructive. I honestly thought that I was talking to a blank wall, that no one was listening to me any more.

I, who am supposed to know more than most about street circuits, had just qualified twenty-first in Detroit. That was not, I knew, my proper place and I was getting afraid that we were falling out of the bottom of the bin. From there it's not far to falling out of the sport altogether, after which everything is over. On the other hand, I had a reasonable race: I was lying fourth, then fifth on lap 47 when I had to retire with an exhaust-pipe failure; it had burned through parts of the car. I was still, at that point, roughly halfway through the season, counting points and I would have been enchanted to get into the points at all.

Keke was not the only driver suffering. Jacques Laffite, though never a champion, had been close enough to get a sniff of the laurels. I saw the like-

able Frenchman the same weekend; his face registered exactly the same disgruntlement. The move to Williams, a top-flight team, had seemed to him manna from heaven after years in the wasteland. His disappointment was all the keener for being set against such expectations. At the end of the year his contract with Williams ended, and Jacques was replaced by Nigel Mansell.

I went through thick and thin with Jacques in those two years. I have really enjoyed working with him though I sometimes thought that after practice he could have put a little more effort into the team instead of taking off for his golf or his tennis. But that's the nature of the man. He does not make waves and I'm afraid that may handicap him; it makes it possible for team to ignore him. I think he has the qualities necessary to be a top driver – when he has a competitive car. But he's been in the game so many years that I'm not sure he's prepared to do the kind of long-range work over several races that it takes to develop a car. He lacks long-term commitment. If the car works, he's quick; if it doesn't, he's less quick.

For what it's worth, I don't think I have that capacity for long-range development either. Apart from one or two things which had nothing to do with his racing, Jacques was always treated very fairly by the team – up to the point when his contract wasn't renewed. By which time he couldn't negotiate a new one. That's the way the system operates.

Two weeks later we were in Dallas where the whole key was the heat. A lot of people came to Dallas feeling beaten ahead of time by the heat. My attitude was to say, 'Ah, what lovely sunshine.' I sat on the pit wall enjoying the sun while others sat in the shade with an ice pack on their heads saying how terrible it was.

The track was new and, frankly, I think FISA should stick to the old rule – which seems to have vanished from the rule book – that there has to be at least one major race on a new circuit before you can have an F1 race.

The freshly laid Dallas track, already crumbling in practice, fell apart badly after a Can-Am race. A driver boycott was in the offing and it took several hours before any of us knew whether there would or would not be a Dallas Grand Prix. As usual, Keke was not a protestor.

My views are fairly simple. No, I wouldn't have had a Can-Am race before an F1 race if the track was already showing signs of breaking up. As an organizer, I would simply have asked myself, 'Which is more important?' But when Sunday morning comes up, and you've had your race, it's too late to do much about it. It was very fortunate that we were able to race at all. As for the boycott, I didn't join it because I was tricked into a strike in South Africa and I don't like being made a sucker twice. But I'm not saying a race should go on, whatever the circumstances. It's easier to back out and say, 'Let's see what happens.' But somewhere along the line I think I'd feel guilty towards my sponsors and towards the crowd. You just don't call a race off at eleven o'clock on a Sunday morning. I'd come a long way to race and whatever the reason you can't call it off at that stage.

I must have been right because I won the race. Did I think beforehand I could win it? Yes. I had thought anyone who survived the race in those conditions was in with a chance. I didn't think I would come up as fast as I did at the beginning, but fairly early on I was running third, then second. The car held together, possibly because of the circumstances. I'll miss Dallas in the calendar because I think it's a very suitable place for a US Grand Prix. The sponsors loved it, television loved it, the whole world loved seeing a race in Dallas. The whole question of giving Dallas a different date was handled very badly on both sides. I hope it comes back.

Although I don't like having favourites, Brands Hatch, which was next, remains the circuit I like best and after my win at Dallas – which always proves that you're competitive – I was on a bit of a high. I could still afford a high in mid-season, particularly in the middle of such a bad season. The team didn't stop working on the car and, every time I went out in it, I thought, 'This time it's going to work.' I knew things were happening; I knew we weren't standing still.

None the less, I remember little about the race at Brands apart from the fact that I qualified fifth and stopped after five laps with a blown turbo. I do remember it as the scene of my one and only slanging match with Frank Williams. As I started walking towards the motor home after the engine had blown, Frank started chasing after me and saying, 'It's not blown, the engine is perfectly all right.' Thank God I'm not a violent man, because that really got my back up. I turned around and said, 'Listen, when I say an engine is blown up it's blown up. I don't want to hear anything else from anybody.' At the time Frank didn't answer me. Two or three minutes later he said, 'You're right.' I respect him for that. Things were hectic, disappointing. Frank is an instinctive racer, a deeply competitive man. If there's anything he can do to keep a car racing he will do it. He's stubborn, too: he might push the car around himself for thirty laps and *then* come to the conclusion that the engine isn't working.

Hockenheim was next; it was another low. It has a long straight and lots of chicanes from which I knew I couldn't exit properly because of the understeer. The whole configuration of the track simply emphasized how bad the problem was and I qualified at the wrong end of the grid, nineteenth. I started the race well but, when I was holding the engine on full throttle, one of the computer sensors broke and said to the computer, 'This idiot has shut the throttle off.' The computer decided that Keke didn't deserve any fuel, so it shut off the fuel supply. Such a small thing. Of course, I didn't know what had happened. All I knew was that I'd qualified badly and had driven well, passing lots of people, and then – disaster – ten laps into the race. I walked back to the pits, feeling sick, and watched the race on television until it got critical to beat the traffic out.

Losing like that was like going from Finland to the tropics and back; it was just too quick from high to low. There was no consolation available. Disappointments will always overcome the joys.

I let myself down for a while, but I can come back up pretty fast. I look forward rather than back.

Looking ahead to Austria, I thought it wouldn't be so bad. The aerodynamic performance of the car was good. I thought it might be a different story, but in fact it was my worst race ever. I've never given up a race because of ill-handling with a mechanically sound car. Ninth on the grid, I pulled in after fifteen laps. Quite simply, I couldn't control the car. I was always in the wrong place. It wasn't because I wasn't enjoying racing any more or because I'd lost interest. But it's very difficult for someone not in the car to understand.

Pulling in like that – with a car that's otherwise OK and the driver saying he can't drive it – is quite a test of the relationship between driver and team. Back in the pits, they don't know that your car is going into a 200-kph right-hander and is deciding instead to go left. They don't know that when it does the same thing five times, it's a bit hard to take. They don't know how dangerous the conflict is: I like to go fast, the car has its own ideas, we don't match.

I know Frank went through a short period of time in which he carefully considered whether relations with Rosberg were worth pursuing, but in the end it worked out satisfactorily. He concluded that they were worth pursuing. The test had been passed. I don't know whether Frank thought I had done right; I know I had. Or did he decide it was better to forget the past and look forward to the next race?

In fact, relations within the team were increasingly strained as bad result followed bad result. But Keke was a valuable property. Other teams, then in the process of picking their drivers for the following year (Monza, two races on, is the traditional slave-market) must have tried to hire Keke away from Williams, despite the fact that Williams had contracted Keke's services for two years. Keke himself must have been sorely tempted to leave.

Zandvoort was a period of deep discussion within the team. I was trying to be both constructive and yet critical about things that I knew were wrong. They weren't just details, like brakes or wheels or suspensions, they were organizational matters. Usually, the team complains that the driver is never available for discussion when they need him; this time, I was complaining that no one would pay attention to me. I don't know to what extent these discussions changed things, but I know that, after the crisis in Austria, we at least got to know each other a little better. The discussions also led to Neal Oatley becoming my engineer instead of Patrick Head, who took on Jacques. There is no deep secret about the decision; we were not communicating well with each other and it was Patrick's decision. Rather than try to improve communications, we decided to pair the engineers and drivers differently. It only lasted for one race, anyway.

I remember Zandvoort as a bad race for me. I qualified seventh and ran out of fuel with two laps left. I was running third and, considering that I'd thrown in the towel the week before, was wondering what to do. If I drove into the pits and said, 'I'm going to run out of fuel,' what would they think? I decided to drive on and try to keep third place, lowering the power. But to stay third when you're being pushed by two Lotuses is no Sunday cruise. In the end, I realized that the tactics I was using to stay in my place weren't going to do me any good anyway because I couldn't possibly finish. I had so little power and Mansell passed me as I dropped out without fuel. F1 matures a man fast.

It takes no imagination to realize that by Monza the atmosphere within the team was electric. Still, the amazing thing is that everyone was still doing his best as far as racing was concerned. At Monza, where I was sixth on the grid, Jacques and I both came in with engine failure within a lap of each other. That didn't exactly help to improve the team's morale. My services had been assigned to Williams for 1985, so there wasn't any point discussing alternative plans; however, it was at Monza that Frank announced that Nigel Mansell was going to join the team. Everyone, inside and outside the team, knew that that was not exactly my wish.

During the year, Keke had had two surprisingly (for him) acerbic run-ins with the British Lotus driver. One was at Detroit and the other at Dallas, where he described Mansell's driving in the race as 'not up to professional standards'. The remark was made in the heat of the moment and came in the wake of considerable publicity about disagreements between Mansell and Peter Warr, the Lotus manager, as well as his team-mate Elio de Angelis. But still, the remark echoed around the tight little world of F1.

People react far too readily to what they read or see on television. The fact is, I've always liked Mansell privately. I criticize only his working relationships. The public takes the remarks to refer to the whole. My objections to Nigel were purely professional. The team was already under considerable stress and I felt Nigel would bring to the team a new factor which was only likely to increase that stress. I knew that there had been tensions around Nigel in F2 and it is no secret that he did not enjoy a perfectly happy relationship within Lotus during 1984. I know Elio de Angelis, Peter Warr and Ducarouge pretty well and, as far as I can see, there is no reason why a driver shouldn't get along well with the people he has to work with. I was concerned for myself. Privately, we get along very well. The human being I can get along with; the professional person I'm not so sure about. And I didn't think we needed any more tension within the team.

Whatever I meant, the result of my stated feelings merely helped to confirm Mansell's joining Williams. I'm sure that somewhere down the line Frank had decided, quite rightly, that he and not Keke Rosberg was running Team Williams. The one time I was asked my opinion by Frank about taking on Mansell, the discussion was perfectly open and calm. Frank asked his Number One driver what he thought, and I told Frank what I thought. Frank listened to me and I'm sure he understood what I was saying. 'You'll get along,' he said. 'It won't be a problem.' To which I say, 'Amen. God, I hope so.' If I expressed any doubts, it is because F1 as a professional sport is hard enough without having a huge personal problem within your working environment. Personal problems are not good fertilizer. They don't lead to a good product.

I don't run Williams Grand Prix. Frank and Patrick do. I am one of the parties involved. It is a fact, and as far as the man Mansell is concerned I have no problem. Nigel is in the team: our job is to get along and do the best we can in 1985. I stress that there is no ill-feeling between Frank and myself on this score; he can take on whom he wants. I just find it curious how little attention in F1 is paid to creating a real *team*. What most of the world sees is just a bunch of individuals dressed in the same colours. In other professional sports, it is readily understood that no individual can conquer the world on his own; that there is a place for teamwork; that the more unified the team, the greater the progress.

Possibly some of Keke's initial apprehension derived from the fact that Frank is a notoriously patriotic Englishman. Would Frank promote Nigel at Keke's expense?

Obviously, I'm aware of Frank the patriot. I think it's an admirable thing to be patriotic. I do not think, however, that Frank's patriotism would ever affect his professional judgment, therefore I would be very surprised if it had any effect at all on what happono in 1905.

The Nürburgring, which was next on the calendar, was recently entirely rebuilt at vast cost. Keke got some stick for being critical of some aspects of the circuit, which he calls 'a very impressive playground'.

I do know this about it: it is the test of how perfect a computer is. The circuit was computer-planned, budgeted and designed, but it still has to be driven on by human beings and men do not necessarily agree with computers. Some aspects of the track are not my cup of tea and I now find driving there just about as exciting as playing a video game on a screen. In its favour, I'll say it's very safe. If you spin, you push the button and the car goes back on the track; you push another button and it goes forward again. I know it has a huge following. The real question is, can it provide good racing? That we'll find out next August if the Ring holds the race and the weather is better. I suppose what I dislike most are the chicanes. Oh why on earth, with all that money and a brand-new circuit, did the computer write in chicanes? Old circuits with their chicanes can fade away, but why put chicanes in when you start from scratch? Before the race, I didn't like the fast chicane at the back, and after I didn't like the one at the start, where a ten-lane road narrows down into one lane.

As for the race, I had a big bang with Senna right at the start which put me out. He flew right over me. When I got out of the car, I asked him what had happened. He said he was hit up the backside by Surer. But when I looked at the pictures after the race, I couldn't find Surer within twenty-seven miles of him; he wasn't even on the same side of the track.

As is obvious, things were not getting better, although I had qualified fourth and was actually looking forward to the race.

After the Ring there was only Estoril left, about which I had fond memories of fantastic races in F2. It was good to go back and see the track has really been changed into a super track for F1 – when they get it right. On the day, it was very muddy from all the construction. It amazes me that we are expected to drive our finely tuned machines on dirty tracks. People have to cope with far more difficult tasks; what's the problem with cleaning up the track properly? In the event, the conditions didn't matter because more changes had to be made. There was zero grip, speeds were kept low, very slow, and nothing bad happened.

There I was without grip and suddenly the car was competitive again from the word go. I had qualified fourth despite a weekend plagued by a host of niggling little technical problems which nearly left me unqualified. I went out with just a few minutes to go. On those occasions, you just have to ignore the problems and do the best you can.

At the start of the race, the Honda seemed to get the idea. Prost missed a shift and I managed a good start and got the lead, though I knew I couldn't hold it for long. After about eight laps, I knew it was all over. The handling had gone. I spoke to Alboreto after the race and he said the same thing: at the beginning the tyres were so good they carried the car, but eventually the car beat the tyres. I was running fourth when I stopped on lap 39, and this time it was not the systems but the engine itself that let go.

A cold look at the balance sheet says I didn't finish a race after Dallas. That makes the situation look worse than it actually was. There were times when we were competitive. When we were, we were completely unreliable. My season was done. It wasn't likely to impress anyone. But overall, even if everything had been working perfectly, the domination of the McLarens was total. And difficult to understand. How is it one car wins twelve races and another, mine, fails to finish the last seven races?

After a terrible season like that, the team has picked up the pieces very bravely. They are very determined to do better in 1985. There is no point in letting your head hang down. If you don't look to the future, you're not going to get anywhere.

Two puzzles remain about 1984 and leave unanswered questions about 1985. Why was the Honda engine, looked on as a salvation after 1983, so unreliable? And, since a new year after a bad season means a new car, why has it taken so long to produce one?

If I weren't worried about the engine, I wouldn't be looking the facts in the face. Engine failures caused me not to finish a race from July to November. But I am sure the Honda people can do it; I know they work very hard at it. As to why the engine didn't work in 1984, I can't answer that. I hope the people who count can. It is probably a matter of details. But I'm not kept informed as to whether they've solved the problems. Drivers can ask; they're not always told. I do know Patrick's been in Japan during the winter. He was very happy when he came back. Obviously he's had some unanswered questions answered.

As to the slowness in developing a new car, I think there are several sound reasons for that. In the first place, Patrick has a very thorough approach to new materials and to new technology. He is not going to commit himself to building a race car until he fully understands the weaknesses, the faults and the virtues of any new material. Secondly, deciding that they were not going to make a carbon-fibre chassis until they could make it in house is a Williams decision, and a very complex one. It is a complicated process and requires heavy investment. That's up to them and I have faith in them: I have to think they know what they are doing.

Williams are typical of F1. F1 is a great business because it has Bernie Ecclestone. Every professional sport is begging for its own Bernie Ecclestone. Bernie comes in for a lot of criticism and I wouldn't know if the critics are right or wrong. I just *know* there isn't anyone else who works as hard or has done so much for the sport. I have to be clever enough to see that, at the end of the day, I profit from it.

It's the same with my own team. I may be critical, but I know they work hard at their jobs and I know they are good at their jobs. In the end I should profit from that.

A deep winter freeze had settled over Europe as we finished talking, Keke and I. But the winter seemed to have gone from his soul. He may say he is no philosopher, but F1 forces an intelligent driver to think. As always with Keke, the thinking had come out positive. His new Lear Jet bestrides the sky with Keke at the controls and the lovely Sina ('As famous in Helsinki as Lady Di in England') is expecting their first child towards the time of Montreal. As Keke said, 'The important things are in place.' I think he's right.

Career Record

1965

Formula K
Finnish Championship   3rd

1966

Formula K
Finnish Championship   1st
Scandinavian Championship   1st

1967

Formula K
Finnish Championship   1st

1968

Formula K
Finnish Championship   2nd

1970

Formula K
Finnish Championship   1st
World Championship   5th

1971

Formula K
Finnish Championship   2nd

1972

Formula Vee 1300
Finnish Championship   2nd
Scandinavian Championship   4th
Finnish VW Cup   1st

1973

Formula Vee 1300
Finnish Championship   1st
Scandinavian Championship   1st
European Championship   1st

1974

Date	Circuit	Country	Car	Result
31 Mar	Aspern	Austria	Bosch-Kaiman	Retired
21 Apr	Österreichring	Austria	Bosch-Kaiman	5
28 Apr	Nürburgring	West Germany	Bosch-Kaiman	4
5 May	Ahvenisto	Finland	FVee 1300	1
19 May	Nürburgring	West Germany	Bosch-Kaiman	Retired
2 Jun	Salzburgring	Austria	Bosch-Kaiman	Retired
9 Jun	Hockenheim	West Germany	Bosch-Kaiman	4
30 Jun	Österreichring	Austria	Bosch-Kaiman	1
14 Jul	Hockenheim	West Germany	FVee 1300	1
14 Jul	Hockenheim	West Germany	Bosch Kaiman	1
21 Jul	Diepholz	West Germany	Bosch-Kaiman	Retired
4 Aug	Nürburgring	West Germany	Bosch-Kaiman	2
11 Aug	Karlskoga	Sweden	Bosch-Kaiman	5
18 Aug	Keimola	Finland	Bosch-Kaiman	2
18 Aug	Keimola	Finland	FVee 1300	2
1 Sept	Avus	West Germany	Bosch-Kaiman	1
8 Sept	Zolder	Belgium	Bosch-Kaiman	1
15 Sept	Norisring	West Germany	Bosch-Kaiman	Retired
22 Sept	Silverstone	England	Bosch-Kaiman	1
29 Sept	Hockenheim	West Germany	Bosch-Kaiman	Retired
3 Nov	Zandvoort	Holland	Bosch-Kaiman	8

1974

		Results		
Races	21			
Results (1st–6th)	14	VW Gold Cup		3rd
Other results	1	Castrol GTX Trophy		2nd
Retirements	6			
Retirements (%)	28.6			

1975

Date	Circuit	Country	Car	Result
31 Mar	Nürburgring	West Germany	Kaiman/Heidegger	1
6 Apr	Aspern	Austria	Kaiman/Heidegger	1
13 Apr	Hockenheim	West Germany	Kaiman/Heidegger	1
27 Apr	Nürburgring	West Germany	Kaiman/Heidegger	Retired
4 May	Sembach	West Germany	Kaiman/Heidegger	Retired
18 May	Salzburg	Austria	Kaiman/Heidegger	3
31 May	Nürburgring	West Germany	Kaiman/Heidegger	1
7 Jun	Anderstorp	Sweden	Kaiman/Heidegger	Disqualified
15 Jun	Mainz-Finthen	West Germany	Kaiman/Heidegger	1
29 Jun	Norisring	West Germany	Kaiman/Heidegger	1
13 Jul	Nürburgring	West Germany	Kaiman/Heidegger	Retired
20 Jul	Diepholz	West Germany	Kaiman/Heidegger	2
3 Aug	Nürburgring	West Germany	Kaiman/Heidegger	Retired
17 Aug	Österreichring	Austria	Kaiman/Heidegger	3
23 Aug	Mainz-Finthen	West Germany	Kaiman/Heidegger	1
31 Aug	Silverstone	England	Kaiman/Heidegger	1
14 Sept	Zolder	Belgium	Kaiman/Heidegger	13
28 Sept	Hockenheim	West Germany	Kaiman/Heidegger	Retired
5 Oct	Watkins Glen	USA	Supernova Super VW	6
9 Nov	Hockenheim	West Germany	Kaiman/Karringer VW 1300	1
9 Nov	Hockenheim	West Germany	Kaiman/Heidegger	1

1975

Races	21		*Results*	
Results (1st–6th)	15		VW Gold Cup	5th
Other results	1		Castrol GTX Trophy	1st
Retirement	4		Super VW German	1st
			Championship	
Retirement (%)	19		Solex Cup	1st
Disqualification	1			

1976

Date	Circuit	Country	Car	Practice	Race result
4 Apr	Nürburgring	West Germany	TOJ Super VW		2
11 Apr	Hockenheim	West Germany	TOJ F201	16	Retired
18 Apr	Thruxton	England	TOJ F201	19	Retired
25 Apr	Sylt	West Germany	VW Sirocco		18
9 May	Vallelunga	Italy	TOJ F201		Disqualified
23 May	Salzburgring	Austria	TOJ F201	22	13
20 Jun	Hockenheim	West Germany	TOJ F201	12	Retired
27 Jun	Rouen	France	TOJ F201	11	4
11 July	Mugello	Italy	TOJ F201	14	Retired
25 Jul	Lago di Pergusa	Italy	TOJ F201		Disqualified
11 Aug	Estoril	Portugal	Chevron	3	Retired
26 Sept	Hockenheim	West Germany	TOJ F201	17	5
10 Oct	Sauerland	West Germany	TOJ F201		1
6 Nov	Hockenheim	West Germany	TOJ F3		2

1976

Races	14	*Result*	
		European Formula 2	
		Championship	10th
Races	25	*Result*	

1977

Date	Circuit	Country	Car	Practice	Race result
3 Jan	Bay Park	New Zealand	Chevron/Hart	1	Retired
8 Jan	Pukekohe	New Zealand	Chevron/Hart	2	1
15 Jan	Manfield	New Zealand	Chevron/Hart	1	1
22 Jan	Teretonga	New Zealand	Chevron/Hart	1	1
29 Jan	Christchurch	New Zealand	Chevron/Hart	1	2
6 Mar	Silverstone	England	Chevron F2	5	Retired
11 Apr	Thruxton	England	Chevron F2	9	Retired
17 Apr	Hockenheim	West Germany	Chevron F2	9	8
1 May	Nürburgring	West Germany	Chevron F2	8	3
15 May	Vallelunga	Italy	Chevron F2	10	12
22 May	Mosport	Canada	Chevron F Atlantic	3	Retired
29 May	Pau	France	Chevron F2	6	11
19 Jun	Mugello	Italy	Chevron F2	5	Retired
26 Jun	Gimli	Canada	Chevron F Atlantic	6	2
3 Jul	Edmonton	Canada	Chevron F Atlantic	3	2
10 Jul	Nogaro	France	Chevron F2	8	13
17 Jul	Westwood	Canada	Chevron F Atlantic	2	1
24 July	Lago di Pergusa	Italy	Chevron F2	1	1
7 Aug	Halifax	Canada	Chevron F Atlantic	4	Retired
14 Aug	San Feliciano	Canada	Chevron F Atlantic	8	Retired

Keke

1977 (*continued*)

Date	Circuit	Country	Car	Practice	Race result
4 Sept	Trois-Rivières	Canada	Chevron F Atlantic	4	Retired
25 Sept	Quebec	Canada	Chevron F Atlantic	2	11
2 Oct	Estoril	Portugal	Chevron F2	7	4
30 Oct	Donington Park	England	Chevron F2	3	2
6 Nov	Suzuka	Japan	Renault F2	3	Retired

1977

Results (1st–6th)	11	European F2 Championship	6th
Other results	5		
Retirements	9	Formula Atlantic	4th
Retirement (%)	36	Formula Pacific	1st
Disqualification	0	Tasman	

1978

Date	Circuit	Country	Car	Practice	Race result
2 Jan	Bay Park	New Zealand	Chevron/Hart	1	1
7 Jan	Pukekohe	New Zealand	Chevron/Hart	2	1
15 Jan	Manfield	New Zealand	Chevron/Hart	2	2
22 Jan	Teretonga	New Zealand	Chevron/Hart	1	2
29 Jan	Christchurch	New Zealand	Chevron/Hart	4	2
4 Mar	Kyalami	South Africa	Theodore F1	24	Retired
19 Mar	Silverstone	England	Theodore F1	11	1
27 Mar	Thruxton	England	Chevron F2	29	Retired
2 Apr	Long Beach	USA	Theodore F1	–	Disqualified
2 Apr	Long Beach	USA	Chevron F Atlantic	6	Retired
9 Apr	Hockenheim	West Germany	Chevron F2	2	8
23 Apr	Vancouver	Canada	Chevron F Atlantic	8	1
30 Apr	Nürburgring	West Germany	Chevron F2	2	2

1978 (*continued*)

Date	Circuit	Country	Car	Practice	Race result
7 May	Monte Carlo	Monaco	Theodore F1	–	Disqualified
14 May	Pau	France	Chevron F2	9	Retired
21 May	Zolder	Belgium	Theodore F1	–	Disqualified
28 May	Mugello	Italy	Chevron F2	9	Retired
2 Jun	Jarama	Spain	Theodore F1	–	Disqualified
4 Jun	Vallelunga	Italy	Chevron F2	5	Retired
11 Jun	Quebec	Canada	Chevron F Atlantic	4	1
17 Jun	Anderstorp	Sweden	ATS F1	23	15
25 Jun	Donington Park	England	Chevron F2	10	1
2 Jul	Paul Ricard	France	ATS F1	26	16
4 Jul	Lime Rock	USA	Chevron F Atlantic	6	4
9 Jul	Nogaro	France	Chevron F2	12	Retired
16 Jul	Brands Hatch	England	ATS F1	22	Retired
23 Jul	Elkhart Lake	Canada	Chevron F Atlantic	10	7
30 Jul	Hockenheim	West Germany	Wolf F1	19	10
7 Aug	Hamilton	Canada	Chevron F Atlantic	3	1
13 Aug	Österreichring	Austria	Wolf F1	25	10
27 Aug	Zandvoort	Holland	Wolf F1	24	Retired
10 Sept	Monza	Italy	Wolf F1	–	Disqualified
24 Sept	Montreal	Canada	Chevron F Atlantic	9	13
1 Oct	Watkins Glen	USA	ATS F1	15	Retired
8 Oct	Montreal	Canada	ATS F1	21	Retired
5 Nov	Mendoza	Argentina	Chevron F2	5	9
12 Nov	Buenos Aires	Argentina	Chevron F2	10	9
19 Nov	Macao	Macao	Chevron F Atlantic	3	Retired

1978

Races	38	*Results*		
Results (1st–6th)	12	European F2	5th	
Other results	9	Championship		
		Formula Atlantic	2nd	
Retirements	12	Formula 1 World	–	
Retirement (%)	31.6	Championship		
Disqualification	5	Formula Pacific	1st	
Disqualification (%)	13.9			

Keke

1979

Date	Circuit	Country	Car	Practice	Race results
9 Feb	Ahvenanmaa Rally	Finland	Ford Escort		7
11 Mar	Mie	Japan	Chevron F2	3	Retired
8 Apr	Hockenheim	West Germany	March F2	3	1
29 Apr	Nürburgring	West Germany	March F2	1	Retired
6 May	Road Atlanta	USA	Scorpion Can-Am	2	1
20 May	Charlotte	USA	Scorpion Can-Am	1	2
3 Jun	Mosport	Canada	Scorpion Can-Am	1	Retired
10 Jun	Mid-Ohio	USA	Scorpion Can-Am	1	2
1 Jul	Dijon-Prenois	France	Wolf F1	16	9
8 Jul	Watkins Glen	USA	Scorpion Can-Am	1	1
14 Jul	Silverstone	England	Wolf F1	14	Retired
22 Jul	Elkhart Lake	USA	Scorpion Can-Am	1	Retired
29 Jul	Hockenheim	West Germany	Wolf F1	17	Retired
12 Aug	Österreichring	Austria	Scorpion Can-Am	12	Retired
19 Aug	Brainerd	USA	Wolf F1	1	Retired
26 Aug	Zandvoort	Holland	Wolf F1	8	Retired
2 Sept	Trois Rivières	Canada	Scorpion Can-Am	2	7
9 Sept	Monza	Italy	Wolf F1	23	Retired
16 Sept	Imola	Italy	Wolf F1	8	6
30 Sept	Montreal	Canada	Wolf F1	26	Disqualified
9 Oct	Watkins Glen	USA	Wolf F1	12	Retired
14 Oct	Laguna Seca	USA	Scorpion Can-Am	1	6
28 Oct	Riverside	USA	Scorpion Can-Am	1	Retired
4 Nov	Suzuka	Japan	March F2	3	3

1979

Races	24	*Results*		
Results (1st–6th)	8	European F2		12th
Other results	3	Championship		
		Can-Am		4th
Retirements	12	Formula 1 World		–
Retirement (%)	50	Championship		
Disqualification	1			
Disqualification (%)	4.1			

1980

Date	Circuit	Country	Car	Practice	Race results
13 Jan	Buenos Aires	Argentina	Fittipaldi F7 F1	13	3
27 Jan	Sao Paulo	Brazil	Fittipaldi F7 F1	15	9
1 Mar	Kyalami	South Africa	Fittipaldi F7 F1	23	Retired
30 Mar	Long Beach	USA	Fittipaldi F7 F1	22	11
4 May	Zolder	Belgium	Fittipaldi F7 F1	21	7
18 May	Monte-Carlo	Monaco	Fittipaldi F7 F1	24	Disqualified
1 Jun	Jarama	Spain	Fittipaldi F7 F1	18	Retired
8 Jun	Ahvenisto	Finland	Chevrolet Camaro	1	2
29 Jun	Paul Ricard	France	Fittipaldi F7 F1	23	Retired
13 Jul	Brands Hatch	England	Fittipaldi F7 F1	26	Retired
10 Aug	Hockenheim	West Germany	Fittipaldi F8/2 F1	8	Retired
17 Aug	Österreichring	Austria	Fittipaldi F8/1 F1	11	16
31 Aug	Zandvoort	Holland	Fittipaldi F7 F1	28	Retired
14 Sept	Imola	Italy	Fittipaldi F8/3	11	5
28 Sept	Montreal	Canada	Fittipaldi F8/2 F1	6	9
4 Oct	Watkins Glen	USA	Toyota Celica		1
5 Oct	Watkins Glen	USA	Fittipaldi F8/3 F1	14	10
19 Oct	Laguna Seca	USA	Lola Can-Am	2	2
26 Oct	Riverside	USA	Lola Can-Am	2	4

1980

Races	19	*Results*	
Results (1st–6th)	6	Formula 1 World Championship	10th
Other results	6		
		Can-Am	12th
Retirements	4		
Retirement (%)	21		
Disqualification	3		
Disqualification (%)	15.8		

1981

Date	Circuit	Country	Car	Practice	Race results
7 Feb	Kyalami	South Africa	Fittipaldi F8/C F1	4	4
15 Mar	Long Beach	USA	Fittipaldi F8/C F1	16	15
29 Mar	Rio de Janeiro	Brazil	Fittipaldi F8/C F1	12	9
12 Apr	Buenos Aires	Argentina	Fittipaldi F8/C F1	8	Retired
3 May	Imola	Italy	Fittipaldi F8/C F1	15	Retired
17 May	Zolder	Belgium	Fittipaldi F8/C F1	11	Retired
31 May	Monte-Carlo	Monaco	Fittipaldi F8/C F1	21	Disqualified
7 Jun	Ahvenisto	Finland	Chevrolet Camaro	5	2
21 Jun	Jarama	Spain	Fittipaldi F8/C F1	15	12
5 Jul	Dijon-Prenois	France	Fittipaldi F8/C F1	17	Retired
19 Jul	Silverstone	England	Fittipaldi F8/C F1	16	Retired
2 Aug	Hockenheim	West Germany	Fittipaldi F8/C F1	25	Disqualified
30 Aug	Zandvoort	Holland	Fittipaldi F8/C F1	27	Disqualified
13 Sept	Monza	Italy	Fittipaldi F8/C F1	28	Disqualified
20 Sept	Mantorp Park	Sweden	Ford Escort	1	3

1981

Races	15
Results (1st–6th)	3
Other results	2
Retirements	5
Retirement (%)	33
Disqualification	4
Disqualification (%)	26.7

1982

Date	Circuit	Country	Car	Practice	Race results
24 Jan	Kyalami	South Africa	Williams FW07	7	5
21 Mar	Rio de Janeiro	Brazil	Williams FW07	3	2
4 Apr	Long Beach	USA	Williams FW07	8	2
9 May	Zolder	Belgium	Williams FW08	3	2
23 May	Monte-Carlo	Monaco	Williams FW08	6	Retired
6 Jun	Detroit	USA	Williams FW08	3	4
13 Jun	Montreal	Canada	Williams FW08	7	Retired
3 Jul	Zandvoort	Holland	Williams FW08	7	3
18 Jul	Brands Hatch	England	Williams FW08	1	Retired
25 Jul	Paul Ricard	France	Williams FW08	10	5
1 Aug	Diepholz	West Germany	BMW-M1		3
8 Aug	Hockenheim	West Germany	Williams FW08	10	3
15 Aug	Österreichring	Austria	Williams FW08	6	2
22 Aug	Ahvenisto	Finland	Chevrolet Camaro	6	Retired
29 Aug	Dijon-Prenois	France	Williams FW08	8	1
12 Sept	Monza	Italy	Williams FW08	7	8
25 Sept	Las Vegas	USA	Williams FW08	6	5

1982

Races	17	*Results*	
Results (1st–6th)	10	Formula 1 World	1st
Other results	1	Champion	
Retirements	4		
Retirement (%)	23.5		

Keke

1983

Date	Circuit	Country	Car	Practice	Race result
13 Mar	Rio de Janeiro	Brazil	Williams FW08	1	Disqualified
27 Mar	Long Beach	US West	Williams FW08	3	Retired
17 Apr	Paul Ricard	France	Williams FW08	16	5
1 May	Imola	Italy	Williams FW08	11	4
15 May	Monte-Carlo	Monaco	Williams FW08	5	1
22 May	Spa	Belgium	Williams FW08	9	5
5 Jun	Detroit	US East	Williams FW08	12	2
12 Jun	Montreal	Canada	Williams FW08	9	4
16 Jul	Silverstone	Great Britain	Williams FW08	13	11
7 Aug	Hockenheim	West Germany	Williams FW08	12	10
14 Aug	Österreichring	Austria	Williams FW08	15	8
28 Aug	Zandvoort	Holland	Williams FW08	23	Retired
11 Sept	Monza	Italy	Williams FW08	16	11
25 Sept	Brands Hatch	Europe	Williams FW08	16	Retired
15 Oct	Kyalami	South Africa	Williams FW08	6	5

1983

Races	15	*Results*		
Results (1st–6th)	7	Formula 1 World Championship		5th
Retirements	3			
Disqualification	1			

1983

Brazil	9th	2nd
S. Africa	2nd	Retired lap 51.
Belgium (Zolder)	3rd	Retired lap 70. Lack of fuel. Finished 4th lying 3rd.
San Marino	3rd	Retired lap 3. Electrical failure.
France (Dijon)	6th	4th
Monaco	10th	5th
Montreal	15th	Abandoned lap 33. Electrical failure.
USA East (Detroit)	21st	Retired lap 47. Turbo failure and fire.

190

1983 (*continued*)

Date	Circuit	Country	Car	Practice Race result
USA West (Dallas)	4th		1st	
Great Britain (Brands Hatch)	5th		Retired lap 5. Turbo failure.	
Germany (Hockenheim)	19th		Retired lap 10. Electrical failure.	
Austria	9th		Retired lap 15. Handling problem.	
Holland	7th		10th. Fuel failure, lap 68.	
Italy (Monza)	6th		Retired lap 8. Engine failure.	
Europe (Nürburgring)	4th		Retired lap 1. Accident.	
Portugal	4th		Retired lap 30. Engine failure.	

1984

Date	Circuit	Country	Car	Practice	Race results
25 Mar	Rio de Janeiro	Brazil	Williams FW09	9	2
7 Apr	Kyalami	South Africa	Williams FW09	2	Retired
29 Apr	Zolder	Belgium	Williams FW09	3	Retired
6 May	Imola	Italy	Williams FW09	3	Retired
20 May	Dijon	France	Williams FW09	6	4
3 Jun	Monte-Carlo	Monaco	Williams FW09	10	5
17 Jun	Montreal	Canada	Williams FW09	15	Retired
24 Jun	Detroit	US East	Williams FW09	21	Retired
8 Jul	Dallas	US West	Williams FW09	4	1
22 Jul	Brands Hatch	Great Britain	Williams FW09	5	Retired
5 Aug	Hockenheim	West Germany	Williams FW09	19	Retired
19 Aug	Österreichring	Austria	Williams FW09	9	Retired
26 Aug	Zandvoort	Holland	Williams FW09	7	10
9 Sept	Monza	Italy	Williams FW09	6	Retired
7 Oct	Nürburgring	Europe	Williams FW09	4	Retired
28 Oct	Estoril	Portugal	Williams FW09	4	Retired

1984

Races	16
Results (1st–6th)	4
Retirements	11